BOWLAND & PE

When I was a boy, my grandfather
said: 'Lad – pick an area and get to know it'.
Arthur Raistrick (1897-1991)
the Dales historian

BOWLAND & PENDLE

W R Mitchell

Smith
Settle

First published in 1993 by
Smith Settle Ltd
Ilkley Road
Otley
West Yorkshire
LS21 3JP

ISBN 1 85825 008 0

British Library Cataloguing-in-Publication Data:
A CIP record for this book is available from the British Library.

Designed, printed and bound by
SMITH SETTLE
Ilkley Road, Otley, West Yorkshire LS21 3JP

For Dorothy and Alan Hemsworth

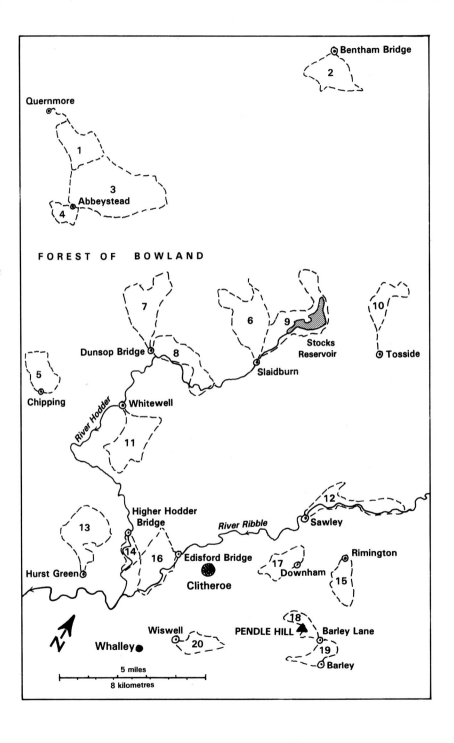

Bentham Bridge

2

Quernmore

1

3
Abbeystead

4

FOREST OF BOWLAND

7

6

9

10

Dunsop Bridge

8

Stocks
Reservoir

Tosside

5

Slaidburn

Chipping

River Hodder

Whitewell

11

Higher Hodder
Bridge

12

River Ribble

Sawley

13

Rimington

14

16

Edisford Bridge

17

Downham

Hurst Green

Clitheroe

15

18

Wiswell

PENDLE HILL

Barley Lane

Whalley

20

19

Barley

5 miles

8 kilometres

CONTENTS

SLAIDBURN
475ft 145m

The starting point of each walk is given in large bold print with the height above sea level

route and way round

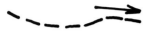

route along a road or lane

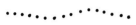

other significant footpaths

rivers and streams with direction of flow

1,000ft 305m

summits and spot heights showing altitude in feet and in metres

selected churches, car parks,

youth hostels and camp sites

PREFACE

The 'Walker's Guide' series, devised by Smith Settle, contains far more than basic directions. Maps give a clear indication of the route. The author devotes much of the text to succinct notes about the chosen area's distinctive landforms, history, folklore, wildlife and flora. Photographs and drawings, many in colour, highlight attractions, including birds, beasts and flowers.

Having written *Three Peaks and Malhamdale* I turned excitedly to an adjacent area, Bowland and Pendle Hill. I thought I knew Bowland well, having visited it regularly for some thirty years. Yet when I came to devise the obligatory twenty walks and followed them up by much walking and looking, I greatly enlarged my experience.

Devising this book has been an indulgence; a matter of personal choice. Each of the twenty walks is circular for the sake of ease. However a 'two car job' would have been a useful arrangement on more than one occasion, such as for the walk from the Trough road, going by Langden Castle to the Bleasdale Fells.

Much of high Bowland is still without public rights of way. Two access areas have been created to enable the energetic visitor to explore some lonely moors, including the tract of country presided over by Wards Stone, the highest point in Bowland.

There are three long distance walks in this area: Witches Way (a 30 miles/48km walk from Rawtenstall to Slaidburn), Ribble Way (a 70 miles/112km walk from Preston to the river's source), and the Pendle Way which is a 45 miles/72km long circular walk. Booklets and leaflets detailing their courses are available locally.

The following Ordnance Survey maps (Landranger Series) cover the Bowland area: 97, 98, 102 and 103. Personally, I ignored Landranger in favour of the Pathfinder Series at 1:25000. Gathering the full Pathfinder set is expensive but the increased scale and the addition of such boundaries as walls is invaluable. The maps to acquire are 650, 659, 660, 669, 670 and 680.

The walks detailed in Bowland and Pendle Hill vary in length from about 3 miles to 14 miles (5 to 22½km) – or from an easy saunter to a seven hour expedition taking in a moorland ridge. The time given with each walk is an underestimation; it does not take into account time off for a snack meal or for photography.

Bowland with Pendle (just across the Ribble Valley) lies within an Area of Outstanding Natural Beauty. The scenery lacks the austere grandeur of the Three Peaks or the Lakeland Fells to the north, but provides the walker with some energetic outings in areas which have retained that tender quality – charm.

Never take Bowland for granted, even in summer. As in all hill country, there is a transient weather system, with rapid changes from good to bad conditions as yet another weather-front sweeps in from the Irish Sea, creating a fell-country cocktail of rain, hail or snow. Pendle is famous for its 'lazy wind' which cuts through you rather than taking the trouble to go round.

For excursions on to high ground, carry weatherproof clothing, wear boots, and have a rucksack with a compass and also, ideally, a warm drink. There is little extra weight in a 'bivvy bag' so pack one in the rucksack.

Before setting out, it is not a bad idea to let someone know where you are going and what time you are likely to be back. To contact the Mountain Rescue Service, telephone 999. The Forest of Bowland Countryside Management Service is based at Carwags, Beacon Fell Country Park, Goosnargh, Preston (tel: 0860 578558). The Bowland Ranger Service shares the same address (tel: 0995 61693).

I am grateful to Bowland estate agents for providing information about their tracts of the district and to the planning department of the Lancashire County Council for information about the administration of the Area of Outstanding Natural Beauty and, in particular, valuable data about the Bowland flora. David Leather's help with the geological section was invaluable. David Binns' artwork gloriously enhances the text. The photographs are by the author.

Mark Whitley, of Smith Settle, was on hand to help at every stage of preparation. His skill ensured an easy transition of the material – text, photographs, drawings and maps – to the printed page.

W R Mitchell
Giggleswick 1993

ACKNOWLEDGMENTS

Thanks are due to the following people for permission to reproduce the undermentioned illustrations:

David Binns, pp15, 16, 25, 45, 49, 67, 77, 84, 88, 92, 93, 96, 105, 107, 113.
Herman Hemingway, pp100, 117.

David Leather drew the maps, geological section and illustration on p4.

All other illustrations were supplied by the author.

PUBLIC TRANSPORT

No public railway service exists within Bowland. Preston or Lancaster are the two handiest main line stations in the west. In the east, stopping places on the Leeds-Carlisle service include Hellifield, Long Preston and Settle.

Bus services are available from Preston and Clitheroe. Buses from Lancaster operate a service in the Lune Valley, with some buses reaching Settle. Another Lancaster service connects the city with Quernmore.

Preston offers regular connections with Chipping and Brock. Information on public transport links is available from the transport enquiry line at Preston (tel: 0772 263333).

Daily buses (except on Sunday) connect Burnley and Nelson with Barley, which is close to Pendle Hill.

TOURIST INFORMATION CENTRES

Clitheroe: 12–14 Market Place	(0200 25566)
Forton: M6	(0524 792181)
Garstang: Discovery Centre, Council Offices	(0995 602125)
Kirkby Lonsdale: 24 Main Street	(05242 71437)
Lancaster: 29 Castle Hill	(0524 32878)
Settle: Town Hall, Cheapside	(0729 825192)
Skipton: 8 Victoria Square	(0756 792809)

INTRODUCTION

In Bowland, you are at the centre of Britain. The Ordnance Survey, using a mathematical computerised technique, fixed the precise spot as an old barn in the middle of a field at Chadswell Hall Farm, Chaigley, in the Ribble Valley.

No public access to the barn exists, but it is good to know it is there. Pilgrims to the heart of Britain had previously gone to Cromwell's Bridge over the Hodder, 2 miles (3km) away. A claim to be at the centre of things had also been made for Whitendale Hanging Stones, near Dunsop Bridge, and Britain's most central payphone stands on the riverside green at Dunsop Bridge, as you will discover if you read the details on the glass panel of the door.

For over 1,000 years Yorkshire had a major share in Bowland and came to within 16 miles (25½km) of the Irish Sea, giving Lancashire a waist like a wasp. This changed with the boundary revision of 1974, when more than 130 square miles (337km²) belonging to the Bowland Rural District Council was transferred into Lancashire. As this guidebook was being compiled, more changes were being proposed.

Bowland's character has not been diluted by bureaucratic exercises. This Area of Outstanding Natural Beauty, comprising 312 square miles (805km²), is an entity, an 'isolated upland area' to quote one description. Bowland's smooth ridges are seen rising from low country round about – from the Lancashire coastal plain in the west, the broad vale of the Lune in the north and the broadening Ribble Valley to the east.

Edmund Vale, writing in 1937 when Bowland was not only isolated but comparatively little-known, described it as 'a semi-detached mass of the western Pennines'. The moors are the backdrop to deeply-incised river valleys, slivers of green among the dun tones of the moors. The Ribble Valley, which had a park-like character before it was grievously lacerated by the Clitheroe and Whalley bypasses, separates Bowland proper from Pendle Hill.

No part of Bowland attains the 2,000 feet (610m) required for mountainhood. The high moors range generally from an elevation of about 600 feet to 1,500 feet (183-457m). Wards Stone, the highest point at 1,863 feet (568m), is no Matterhorn, being but the culminating feature of Littledale Fell.

Bowland and Pendle, at the edge of the East Lancashire conurbation and not far from the West Yorkshire towns, are within an hour's car ride of some five million people, yet the area has emerged from the changeful years with its landscape unsullied and its heritage intact.

The Bowland skyline often takes on strange forms; a consequence of the weathering of gritstone outcrops. In 1964, at the time of Bowland's designation as an Area of Outstanding Natural Beauty, 40,000 acres (16,200ha) were specified as 'open country', including the grouse moors of Harden, Sykes, Brennand, Whitendale and Lamb Hill. They resemble the hills of Scotland in their rich tones, 'blockiness' and wall-less nature. It is, as one landowner says, 'all open space'.

The moors, with their grouse stocks, have had their privacy zealously guarded by landowners and gamekeepers. Lancashire County Council have negotiated access areas with the owners and occupiers of some 3,260 acres (1320ha) of unspoilt country.

Access areas do not establish rights of way and are closed on specified days, such as the start of the grouse-shooting in August. Such areas may also be put out of bounds if there is a high fire risk. Maps and byelaw/restriction notices are posted at the main access points. Country rangers patrol the access areas. A leaflet, published by the county estates surveyor at Winckley House, Winckley Square, Preston, can be obtained at information centres in Bowland.

The fells which now can be visited include some with grand-sounding names – Clougha Pike and Ward Stone, Fairsnape and Saddle Fell, Wolf Fell and Parlick Pike, the last four comprising the Bleasdale Fells and the last-named appealing to enthusiasts of the sport of hang-gliding. They harness the power of the updraught and hover above the bare ridge in multi-coloured splendour.

Newcomers to Bowland, moving into their converted barns or redundant farmsteads, encounter a characterful and independent native-born people. A fourteenth-century Abbot of Whalley referred to the Bowland hillfolk as being 'few, intractable and wild'.

Bowland is generally a dark landscape. Davis and Lee wrote in 1878:

'The great forest of Bowland is for the most part pleasant agricultural country, strong ploughlands and rich pastures. There are wide expanses of unenclosed moor which cannot have altered in spirit since the days when the area was the hunting ground of the de Lacys.'

The Area of Outstanding Natural Beauty is much larger than many people suppose, extending northwards into Lunesdale. View the district from the west, as from the M6, and you see a blue-grey smudge on the horizon; beyond is Shangri-la. The approach from the Wenning Valley, to the north, is undramatic but full of promise. From Clapham, a road ascends in a series of easy gradients up the side of Burnmoor to Bowland Knotts, which are like gritstone teeth on a peaty gum.

The approach from Bentham has a highlight in a roadside erratic (ice-borne boulder) known as the Great Stone of Fourstone, so monstrous it has steps cut up the side (*walk 2*). Beyond, the road crosses an unexceptional tract of fell country, only to come alive again when it passes the base of the Cross of Greet, with the glimmer of Stocks Reservoir seen against conifer plantations and heathered hills.

From the Ribble Valley, between Settle and Gisburn, the bastions of Bowland are green, with flat-topped Whelpstone Crag as a focal point (*walk 10*). A view towards Bowland from the Nick of Pendle, to the south, reveals ridge upon ridge, moor upon moor, like waves in a petrified sea.

Bowland is dissected by the tributaries of the rivers Lune (to the north-west) and Hodder (flowing to the south-east and joining the Ribble). The several western rivers – Wyre, Calder and Brock – descend steep scarps and then make a quick dash to the Irish Sea.

Clitheroe, the principal market town, has a name which is said to derive from Cled-dwr, relating to two limestone knolls, plus the element 'how' – meaning the place of the rocky promontory. Several villages are distinguished by having, as a suffix, the words '-in-Bowland'.

A few Bowland and Ribblesdale names which intrigue visitors include Cowark, Tosside, Grindleton and Dinkley, the latter being a remote parish between Dinkley Brook and the Ribble, surely the resort of fairies or elves. The flavour of Old Bowland is found in such a name as Staple Oak Fell.

The writer Edmund Vale, whose father was Rector of Slaidburn for a short time, referred to the Forest of Bowland as 'a strange and desolate area with a singularly beautiful heart – at Slaidburn'. In his father's time, it was reckoned to be the second largest parish in England. Vale remarked:

'The fells stand round it on every side. To the north they range for about fourteen miles and there is no road through. To the west there is a long road to Lancaster (about twenty miles)

The Trough of Bowland, where the old road to Lancaster climbs through a heathered area. Nervous travellers who intended to take the Trough route would go into the church at Whitewell and pray for a safe journey.

through the sinister moorland pass called the Trough of Bowland, about which, when I was a boy, tales of highwaymen were still alive, and folk-memory still dwelt on the herd of wild cattle that used to roam the old forest.'

Vale wrote of chilling journeys by the rectorial wagonette in winter, adding:

'But Slaidburn was a fairyland in the summer. The river Hodder poured into the village over a fantastic limestone staircase of petrified corals and then wound smoothly through green lawns and parklands. And it went on winding and winding through splendid country where the true wild maidenhair, the lily-of-the-valley and the globe-flower grew, till it found a way through the wall of the fells and by the wooded gorge of Whitewell.'

The Duchy of Lancaster, which owns 5,500 acres (2,227ha) of Bowland along the Hodder Valley, traces its beginnings to the time when Edmund, son of Henry III, was given the 'county, honour and castle' of Lancaster and also the title Earl of Lancaster. Edmund's grandson Henry was created Duke of Lancaster in 1351 and the County of Lancaster became a 'County Palatine' because of special dukal rights. The monarch is toasted in Lancashire as 'The Queen, Duke of Lancaster'.

Lancaster Castle was the destination, by way of the Trough route, of Bowland and Pendle folk who had fallen foul of the law, including John Paslew, Abbot of Whalley, summoned to answer

The sign of the Witches Way, Pendle. Most of the seventeenth century witches lived to the south of Pendle Hill.

a charge of treason through his association with the Pilgrimage of Grace, a northern rising at the time of the seventeenth-century Dissolution of the Monasteries (*walk 20*).

In the seventeeth century, the Trough road was also the route taken to convey the celebrated Pendle Witches to imprisonment, trial and execution at Lancaster. Pendle will be forever associated with this motley group of miscreants, among them Old Demdike and Chattox, who wandered about the Pendle area begging. If their pleas for help were refused, they were inclined to cast a spell.

In the case of John Law, a pedlar of Colne, this led to him having what appears to have been a stroke, which brought the Pendle women into disrepute and also led to their appearance before a local magistrate, accused of witchcraft.

He heard of a witchly gathering at Malkin Tower, the site of which has been forgotten. The women were rounded up and imprisoned. They were hanged from a specially built gibbet on the 20th August 1612. (See the exhibition about the Pendle Witches at the Pendle Heritage Centre, Park Hill, Barrowford, Nelson, BB9 6JQ. Tel: 0282 695366.)

The summit of Pendle, at 1,831 feet (557m), attracts a crowd of witch-spotters at midnight on Hallowe'en. The hill provides the southern part of this area with a strong focal point. In the words of Richard James, a seventeenth-century parson, Pendle stands 'rownd cop, survaiying all ye wilde moore lands'. You will see Pendle during several of the walks. What looks razor-edged from valley level is revealed, to those who climb the hill, to be an extensive plateau. Walking on the hill itself is good fun – if the weather is moderate (*walk 18*).

On the chillest of winter days, a wind across Pendle seems to be questing for the marrow of your bones. An eighteenth-century commentator described Pendle as 'a vast black mountain which is the morning weather glass of the country people'. Local people say that 'if you can see Pendle, it's going to rain; if you can't see Pendle – it's raining'.

On at least three occasions in recorded times, the sides of the hill have been lacerated by water brasts (eruptions). One who witnessed such a phenomenon in 1669 recorded 'a mighty torrent gushing out in such quantities and so suddenly that it made a breast a yard high and continued running for about two hours'.

Pendle, this tabular hill with a sheer, smooth form, has kept its shape and size because of a summit layer of weather-resisting gritstone, a dark brown rock. The hill looks from a distance like an upturned boat.

Pendle is many things to many people. It gave its name to a forest which extended from Pendle to Colne and covered almost 13,000 acres (5,300ha). In the old days, the hill was often written down as Penhull. The name is derived from the Celtic pen, to which was added an English word for hill, being abbreviated to 'Pendle'. So if you utter the name Pendle Hill, you are using the topographical term no less than three times.

ROCKS AND THE LANDSCAPE

Bowland has been studied by geologists since the early part of last century, but comparatively little of geological interest has been published. An exception is the strata of the Clitheroe area. These are sediments laid down under marine conditions during the Carboniferous period which began about 360 million years ago. Limestones were, in turn, overlaid by the Bowland Shales (from ancient muds) and Pendle Grit (from deposits of sand).

These thick sediments were deposited in the Bowland (or Craven) Basin. Compared with the classic Settle area – north of the Craven Faults on the Askrigg block – the Bowland sediments are very thick. They have more muds than limestones, which are often found to be impure or muddy.

Also the strata are more disturbed. Of the folding, the upfolds or anticlines are the most noticeable. These bring the deeper rocks (which here are limestones) to the surface.

Folds in the Strata The main feature of Bowland and Pendle is the Clitheroe Anticline. The town stands near the heart of this broad geological feature, with Pendle Hill forming the south-eastern limb and Waddington Fell the north-western limb.

The anticline brings limestone to the surface, as evidenced by the sight of a line of large conical limebanks (often referred to as reef knolls) which are rich in fossils.

Near Slaidburn, rare fossil trilobites are found in the impure limestones. Trilobites are among the last of a long line of these engaging little fossils and they became extinct by the end of the Carboniferous period.

The oldest limestone is the Chatburn Limestone, in the core of the anticline. This grey-blue limestone is over 1,200 feet (360m) thick. Some of it has been exposed in local quarries.

Clitheroe Reef Knolls An old couplet declares:

'Worsaw, Warren, Ridge and Crow;
Four limestone knolls all in a row.'

The old part of Clitheroe stands on an elongated limestone knoll, with a castle at one end and the parish church at the other. In between lies an attractive main street (*walk 16*).

In line with the Clitheroe knolls are Salt Hill, Crow Hill, Warren Hill and Warsaw Hill. They lie close to the anticlinal axis, with three more to the east. Coplaw, which is a little out of line to the north, is composed of a darker limestone.

Some of the knolls are up to 1,000 feet (305m) thick; their prominence in the limestone is a consequence of their having been surrounded by the more easily-eroded mudstones of the Worston Shale group. Three other knolls are Gerna, Sykes and Twiston.

The limestone of the reef knolls is a creamy-grey rock, consisting largely of the remains of crinoids, brachiopods and corals which in prehistory drew nourishment by 'filter-feeding' on plankton in a shallow tropical sea. Or, as the writer of a guide to Salthill Quarry has it, when describing this important geological exposure: 'this richly fossiliferous limestone is typical of sheltered conditions where the dense population of crinoids lived in an environment of warm shallow water and gentle currents'.

In Bowland, because of the folding in the strata, limestone inliers ('windows' through to older rocks below) are visible in the valleys of Sykes, Brennand and Whitendale (*walk 7*).

The Clitheroe knolls vary in size but all contain fossils giving us an insight into the marine life of Lower Carboniferous times (*walk 17*). The fossils include crinoid stems

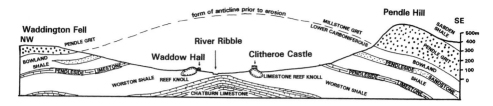

A geological section across the Clitheroe Anticline.

(which are common as fossils) and the so-called 'crinoid heads' (a very rare fossil survival of the animal itself, which was related to the starfish and sea urchin). Clitheroe, and especially Coplow, is one of the few places where they have been well-preserved.

The Clitheroe reef knolls have been quarried for cement on a large scale, the twin chimneys of the Ribble Cement works being visible over a wide area. At Salthill, on the edge of Clitheroe, quarrying has provided us with an insight into this string of reef knolls and their associated rocks.

At Salthill Quarry, which is owned by the Ribble Valley Borough Council, a geology trail has been established. Some beds of limestone are immensely deep, and when the Clitheroe-Whalley bypass was made, workmen had to cut through 60 feet (18m) at Chatburn.

Bowland Shales These are a thick series of black shales with occasional bands of limestone and sandstone. They contain the fossils of shellfish, which were at home on a muddy sea bottom and were mainly free-swimming goniatites (They are all-important in dating the strata because they evolved rapidly and are quite common). Also found are thin-shelled bivalves.

Some of the black shales are highly organic and contain large proportions of petroleum. Others hold small amounts of uranium.

The cloughs (ravines) in the shales on the northern flank of Pendle Hill are classic locations for fossil goniatites.

Pendle, which is flat-topped, consists of a particularly thick and tilted layer of Pendleside Sandstones, reposing in the Bowland Shales.

Millstone Grit Pendle has a hard, impervious cap of millstone grit which has protected underlying softer rocks from rapid weathering (*walk 18*). Longridge Fell (*walk 13*) has also kept its shape well. Minerals in the Millstone Grit show it to be the erosion product of a granite, not unlike that in the present-day Cheviots.

In Bowland the horizons are low and the ridges sparse. The gritstone moors which give so much character to the district have a coverlet of peat, heather and mosses. On the exposed ridges, the outcropping Millstone Grit has been sculptured by the wind to form strange shapes, as on Wolfhole Crag and Wards Stone (*walk 3*).

New Red Sandstone A bed of this rock appears in the riverbed of the Ribble just below Waddow Hall. Here are three small patches, which filled the hollows. The limestone below has been reddened by contact with the red sandstone above.

The Ice Age Bowland's appearance owes much to the abrasive character of glacial ice. During the Ice Age, sheets of ice from the Lake District over-rode Bowland Knotts and created the broad basin of the upper Hodder Valley (*walk 9*). The Ribblesdale Ice Sheet was a sculpturing influence on Pendle,

The sea floor of a Clitheroe reef knoll in Lower Carboniferous times (330 million years ago).

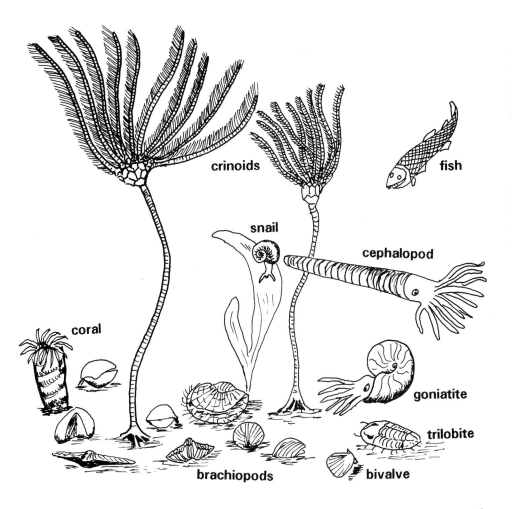

3

The remains of a limestone knoll near Dunsop Bridge, in the valley of the Hodder.

Bowland Knotts, a gritstone outcrop which is a splendid viewpoint for the upper Hodder.

4

severely eroding the north-eastern part of the hill.

Ice gouged out other valleys and plastered slopes up to about 600 feet (180m) with a geological mush called boulder clay, which was deposited beneath the ice. The melting of the ice revealed smooth hills known as drumlins. (A classic area for which is beside the Ribble Valley near Hellifield.) The celebrated Trough of Bowland (*walk 7*) and also Cliviger, near Burnley, were glacial spillways, along which passed a torrent of meltwater.

Bowland's aforementioned 'strong ploughlands and rich pastures' are part of the glacial heritage. The drift soils of the lower slopes are poorly drained, being high in clay content. Bowland never truly dries out, the clay soils staying damp and yielding excellent grazing for livestock even in a dry summer.

I sometimes recite my adaptation of a Cleveland couplet:

'Bowland in the clay;
Take two boots, bring one away . . .'

The ice cleared about 10,000 years ago to be succeeded by tundral conditions.

Climate The prevailing wind being westerly, and Bowland having a close proximity to the sea, the summers tend to be cool and cloudy and the winters and springs quite mild. The most memorable snowfalls, notably 1947 and 1962, occurred at the time of a north-east wind when there was a Continental 'high'. The annual average rainfall in the Bowland valleys is about 50 inches (1,270mm) and on the fell tops may be over 70 inches (1,780mm).

MAN AND THE LANDSCAPE

During the Bronze Age, an improvement in the climate led to a spread of families from the free-draining limestone areas on to the gritstone. Burials of this period have been found on Waddington Fell. At Bleasdale, a small community lived within a palisade consisting of oak posts, their positions now indicated by concrete pillars. Archaeologists found a mound containing a stone-lined chamber with cremation urns.

Bronze Age pottery was found in the Fairy Holes (caves) near Whitewell. These would form a foul-weather sanctuary for an early people who, if they slew something as large and succulent as a deer, hit the culinary jackpot. Among the remains in the Fairy Holes were animal bones which had been pounded to extract the marrow as food.

The few scattered families were semi-nomadic. They cleared the land with the slash-and-burn technique that led eventually to settled farming and followed game tracks through wooded areas. On higher ground were major trade routes, some doubtless connected with Ireland.

The Romans, in their northward progress, encountered a confederation of Iron Age tribes called the Brigantes. Forts and roads were built to police the hill areas of the north-west. The Romans had a direct, no-nonsense approach to road-building. A major road developed through the Ribble Valley was part of the route connecting York with Chester. A fort and civil settlement at Ribchester bore the unwieldy Roman name of Bremetennacum.

Ribchester's importance lay in its strategic position at the junction of two roads. It was connected with Lancaster and another Roman road went northwards from Slaidburn (*walk 6*) to a ford across the Wenning at Bentham, thence to Overburrow near Kirkby Lonsdale.

Roman remains are scanty but important. A hoard of nearly 1,000 Roman coins was found near Downham. A ceremonial helmet, complete with mask, came to light at Ribchester. The helmet reclines in the British Museum, but a replica is one of the exhibits in the small museum of Roman objects adjoining the church at Ribchester – a church which occupies the site of the old temple of Septimus Severus.

Angles, arriving from the east in the sixth or early seventh centuries, were a lowland people, founders of villages named with the suffix 'tun', 'ham' and 'ing', all meaning a homestead or a farm, as in Newton and Easington. Anglian folk also put down family roots at Slaidburn and Whitewell. The River Ribble – possibly derived from the Old English ripel, or boundary – may have been the division between the Anglian kingdoms of Northumbria and Mercia.

The Angles introduced into Bowland the terms clough (ravine) and croft (a small enclosure). These industrious people used their greater manpower and heavier tools to make inroads into the wild wood. The cleared land was farmed. Remoter cloughs were unexploited because of their steep sides and tangle of vegetation.

Vigorous Christian witness led to the appearance of preaching crosses (as at Whalley) and, in due course, thatched churches appeared. An Anglian settlement at Clitheroe was little more than a group of wooden buildings on the knoll where the castle keep now stands.

The Norse-Irish folk who arrived from the west some time after AD 900 were generations removed from their Scandinavian forebears. Emigrants had sailed their long boats to the Northern Isles, then southwards through the Hebrides to Ireland (where many of them married red-haired Irish lasses), and to the Isle of Man.

Some Norsefolk, arriving in Bowland, were thinly spread about the upper dales and the hill land. The limits of their settlement are indicated by the use of the word 'fell' for hill, the most southerly case being Longridge Fell. The new settlers cleared land and established forest clearings or thwaites, and tended cattle and sheep.

Saetrs – high grazings used in summer – enabled the forerunners of our hill farmers to take advantage of the flush of grass on the hills, while the fields around the winter home grew grass to be cut for hay and stored as winter fodder.

Important Norse landowners had their names incorporated in placenames, such as *Batheraghes* – 'Bathar's hill farm' now rendered as Beatrix. Bathar had an *abyr* (homestead) near what is now Slaidburn. The site is now occupied by the house called Dunnow.

Among the Norse names still used in Bowland are beck (stream), gill (ravine), slack (hollow), garth (enclosure), keld (spring or well) and laithe (a barn). The suffix 'laithe' is to be found on the name of almost every farm by the moor-edge road between Slaidburn and the Cross of Greet, to the north.

In Norman times, Roger de Poictou selected an impregnable site for a castle at Clitheroe (*walk 16*). Roger had vast possessions between the Ribble and Mersey. By now, the nuclei of many Bowland villages were established, with Earl Tostig as a major overlord, having his manor at Grindleton. Settlements had sprung up at West Bradford, Waddington, Bashall and Mitton.

The *Domesday* scribes included Bowland under Gretlintone (Grindleton), where Tostig had thirty-eight carucates of land, a caracute being the amount of land for which eight oxen was a requisite team. On the Bowland clays the acreage would be lower than the northern average of 120 acres (50ha).

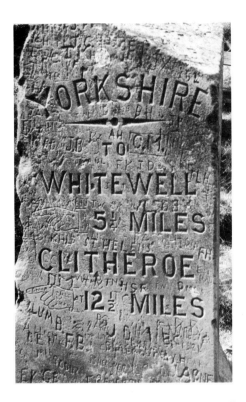

A detail from the County Stone, which may still be seen in the Trough of Bowland. The stone became redundant with local government reorganisation in 1974.

The twelfth century saw a period of Norman benevolence, when notable families – anxious to have a stake both in this world and the next – granted land to the church. The Abbot of Kirkstall was given a 'horse-close at Woodhows in Slayborn' to which the Hammerton family supplied twenty loads of hay a year.

Monks from Fountains Abbey near Ripon settled at Salley, now more popularly known as Sawley, in the Ribble Valley (*walk 12*). What is now a well-farmed landscape was in monastic times such a barren and rainy area that Matilda de Percy, daughter of the founder, augmented their income with the

From about 1250 the chief court of the Forest of Bowland was held at the Hark to Bounty, Slaidburn. An upper room is still furnished with oak benches and a dock.

gift of three churches. Salley was said to have been established in 'a foggy and rainy country ... When the standing crops are already white unto harvest they ordinarily rot in the stalk'.

Conditions here further deteriorated in 1296, when a community of Cistercians from Cheshire settled at Whalley. They took prime salmon out of the Ribble and, through their purchase of grain, butter, cheese and salt, created an inflationary situation. Whalley achieved pre-eminence in the district.

In the twelfth century, the Forest of Bowland was granted to Robert de Lacy, or Lascy, whose emblem was three luces (pikes). Gisburn and Bolton-by-Bowland came under Percy control. Clitheroe had developed from a hamlet originally named *Cled-dwr*, to which

the Saxons added *how*, the whole name being 'the place at the rocky promontory'. Clitheroe became a place of importance following the building of a Norman castle, receiving its first charter from Henry de Lacy in 1177.

The Norman lord hunted in the Forest of Bowland, the word forest being derived from the French word *foras*, meaning land set apart for hunting. It (The Forest of Bowland) was an administrative rather than a physical description; not all would have been covered by trees. The forest laws protected the area for the privileged few and created what was in effect a nature reserve.

Bowland's forest extended from Clitheroe to Bowland Knotts in the north and from Chipping to Bolton-by-Bowland in the east. In 1274, the Royal Forest of Bowland was divided into four wards – Sclatbournewarde (Slaidburn), Baxholfwarde (Bashall), Chepynwarde (Chipping) and Harropwarde (Harrop).

Defining its precise boundaries raised some problems, and disputes occurred. Natural features like streams were boundary markers, such as near Wolfhole Crag where the division occurred 'as heaven water deals'. The Cross of Greet, beside the old route from Slaidburn to Bentham, was a marker in otherwise featureless terrain.

Historically, the most important route is that which climbs to 1,000 feet (300m) at the Trough of Bowland, linking the Hodder Valley with Wyresdale and providing a direct route to Lancaster. Travellers passed the County Stone (Lancashire/Yorkshire) between Blaze Moor (1,385 feet/422m) and Whin Fell (1,565 feet/477m).

It is a wild route and (so it is said) medieval travellers heading for the Trough slipped into the church at Whitewell to pray for safe deliverance during the journey (*walk 11*).

Bowland was hunted over by the Lord of the Honour of Clitheroe, who held his forest or 'woodmote' court at Whitewell until 1322, when a royal forest was established under Edward II, who does not appear to have hunted here. (In 1348 the land was part of the Duchy of Lancaster and so it was to remain until, in 1661, Charles II granted it to General Monck, Duke of Albemarle. It was re-absorbed into the Duchy of Lancaster in the twentieth century when George VI bought the Whitewell Estate.)

The life of the old forest was characterised by vaccaries (cattle ranches), the red and fallow deer being restricted to *launds* (Old French for pastureland) except when some animals were released on hunt days.

In Bowland, a *laund* was a large park surrounded by a ditch, palings or thorn hedges. Parks existed at New Launde and Radholme, on opposite sides of the Hodder at Whitewell (*walk 11*). Another was situated at Leagram, in the Chipping ward (*walk 5*). Such a park was also grazed by horses and cattle.

The cattle kept at the vaccaries were shaggy, black, long-horned beasts, which had free range on the fell and were rounded up if the weather deteriorated or some culling was necessary. Cattle were numerous in Bowland and also in Pendle Forest. In 1295-6 the eleven Pendle vaccaries had a total of 907 animals – bulls, cows, steers, heifers, yearlings and calves.

The cowkeeper of 700 years ago lived in a booth (a Norse term for a farmhouse). Two of the cowkeepers, 'Henry sone of Kitte' and 'Robert Attebrigge', tended the lord's stock and their income came from the milk, from which they made butter and cheese. As herd-replenishment took place, the old stock was removed by 'Simon the geldherd'.

As the vaccary system declined towards the end of the fourteenth century, some ranches were let out for rent. The 'booths' were the nuclei of Pendle hamlets and villages.

Richard and John Parker, who had taken their surname from their occupation as keepers of Radholme, leased the vaccary of Browsholme in 1393 and eventually purchased the property. The hall they built was enlarged by their descendants. Descendants of the Parkers are still associated with Browsholme, which is pronounced 'Brooze-em' (*walk 11*).

During the fifteenth-century Wars of the Roses, which were not national wars but protracted and tedious squabbles between two rival families, Henry VI escaped from certain disaster at the Battle of Hexham and went into hiding at the home of the Pudsays in Bolton-by-Bowland (*walk 12*).

Henry, a scholarly but occasionally mad monarch, enjoyed the hospitality of the Pudsay family, who had been associated with the village since John de Pudesay settled here in 1349. After staying for some months, the king moved on and was apprehended as he crossed the stepping stones at Brungerley by the Talbots from Basham, who were prominent Yorkists.

The hapless king was made to ride to London, his legs being tied to the stirrups and his face turned towards the horse's tail. He died while being imprisoned in the Tower.

In 1507, Henry VII abolished the forest laws as they related to Bowland and other tracts in the area. Land was now available for development. By the end of the century, small farms had been enlarged and moorland reclamation was under way.

Bowland Billmen, to quote one of the contingents mentioned in an old Craven

Newchurch, close to Pendle. The oval feature below the clock is said to represent the all-seeing eye of God.

poem, joined 'a band of lusty lads erect, from Penigent to Pendle Hill' who in 1514 followed Lord Clifford to a decisive English victory against the Scots at Flodden Field.

When Henry VIII ordered the dissolution of the monasteries, in 1536, a vainglorious objection by Northern folk resulted in a rising which became known as the Pilgrimage of Grace, for which a monk of Sawley Abbey (*walk 12*) composed a special hymn, including the words:

> 'Christ crucified
> For Thy wounds wide
> Us commons guide
> That pilgrims be.'

The pilgrimage failed and the hangman was busy, his customers including Stephen Hammerton, Nicholas Tempest and the abbots of Sawley and Whalley. The hangman at Lancaster had a busy time in 1612 when some misguided old ladies from Pendle, who had been tried and found guilty as witches, were hanged at Lancaster Castle.

It was a period when James VI of Scotland became James I of England; he was fascinated by witchcraft, and his obsession and book on the subject made the topic of general interest. It was this superstitious fear of the witches Demdike, Chattox and the others from Pendle country which led to their presentation before a magistrate, Roger Nowell of Read Hall, and the Lancaster trial where their guilt was confirmed.

Also found guilty with them was Alice Nutter, a gentlewoman and devout Catholic, who lived at Roughlee. It is now suspected that when she was said to have attended a witchly gathering she was, indeed, taking part in mass, the celebration of which was then forbidden.

In the sixteenth century, Queen Mary granted a charter establishing a grammar school in Clitheroe. In that same century, penal laws prohibited Catholic schools, so the Jesuits founded a Catholic college at Saint

Hammerton Hall near Slaidburn is a particularly fine Elizabethan house, with mullioned windows. Inside is a stone spiral staircase.

Omer, across the English Channel. The college was to be transferred to Stonyhurst during the nineteenth century, when times were more enlightened (*walk 13*).

During the Civil War (1642-51), Cromwell stayed at Stonyhurst – then the home of the Shireburns – and, having a dread of strange beds, he slept on a table, placing his sword and pistols beside him (*walk 13*). When the dust settled on the Civil War, the castle at Clitheroe was among many fortified buildings which were rendered unusable.

New religious ideas were stirring. George Fox, the founder of Quakerism, 'moved to sound the day of the Lord', climbed Pendle Hill in 1652 and had a vision of a people who were to be gathered (*walk 18*). During the

Great Ejectment from the Church of England of clergymen who would not subscribe to restrictive laws, those who found new homes in Bowland turned it into a bastion of Nonconformity.

In the settled times of the late seventeenth and early eighteenth centuries, when families had money and the confidence to built for posterity, conscious that their sons could inherit and hold their properties, Bowland acquired its attractive stone halls and farms. A particularly grand development at this time was the re-fronting of Bashall Hall (*walk 16*).

The 'fellside economy' was developed by a proud and independent people. Harrop Hall, near Slaidburn, was greatly improved by the Leigh family, who set the date 1719 above the door. The building has long been a farmhouse but an ostentatious feature still remains – a stone ball on a plinth on either side of the massive garden gate.

Bowland and the Pendle countryside were ransacked for minerals by generations of miners who are now collectively known as 'T'owd man'. Their spoil heaps hold traces of both pink and white barite (barium sulphate), quartz, fluorspar, galena (lead ore) and calomine (zinc ore).

Of the several mines, one at Sykes, near the Trough of Bowland, was especially productive. A dwelling at the roadside between here and Dunsop Bridge has the name Smelt Mill, and to this mill came galena from several mines, including one at Brennand, over the hill, where the veins had been intercepted via bell-pits, shafts and a day-level driven in from the foot of the hill (*walk 7*).

Some of the leadmines were especially rich in silver, as William Pudsay, Squire of Bolton-by-Bowland, realised at his mine at 'Skeleron', near Rimington (*walk 15*). William forged coins which became known locally as 'Pudsay's Shillings'.

In the nineteenth century, the industrialisation of the nearby Lancashire valleys drew families from Bowland to the emergent textile towns. Land management in Bowland became less intensive than it had been.

The old Bowland squirearchy, augmented by the 'new rich' of the Industrial Revolution, was to endure many social changes. Sport was important, and the quarry included grouse, pheasant, partridge and hare. Whereas most estates were noted for their grouse, Knowlmere, under Judge Peel, had a relatively small grouse moor but abundant copses and fields for pheasants and partridges (*walk 8*).

The heyday of the big Bowland estates was before the 1914-18 war. Thereafter, the landowners could no longer rely on a large, inexpensive pool of rural labour and had to allocate much of their income to paying taxes.

Grouse-shooters used to walk to the moor. An octogenarian recalls:

'We walked up; we walked down; we went home and next morning we walked up to the moor again . . . Now the shooters are transported in Land Rovers.'

A particularly large Bowland estate, centred on Abbeyfield, is owned by the Duke of Westminster. The estate extends over 19,500 acres (7,900ha).

Many moors are associated with the waterworks and are leased to syndicates. North West Water has become a major landowner in Bowland and the area south of Pendle, and waterworks installations indicate that much of Bowland's rainfall eventually flows through Lancashire towns, including those on the thirsty Fylde coast.

The main industries in Bowland today are farming and tourism. Many farms have diversified by offering 'bed and breakfast' facilities to visitors.

Lancashire's first country park was opened at Beacon Fell (873 feet/266m) in 1970, being one of the first such parks to be officially recognised by the Countryside Commission. Situated at the western edge of Bowland, eight miles (13km) north of Preston, Beacon Hill is far different in appearance and concept from the urban park with its trim lawns and flowerbeds. It covers 185 acres (75ha) of rough moorland and woodland. Through leaflets, displays and well-marked walks, it provides a splendid introduction to Bowland traditions and natural history.

Ordinary folk, with the greater mobility provided by the car, and using much-improved roads such as the motorways, now flood into parts of Bowland during the holiday season. The recreational pressures are great. Bowland, once a quiet, unhurried sort of place, now has its 'honeypots' like Slaidburn, Dunsop Bridge and Chipping,

Silage time, near Dunsop Bridge. Silage is grass cut and transported from the meadow in a wilted but still green state, as opposed to sun- and wind-dried hay.

where life in summer is all of a bustle. Overall, Bowland is a quiet district but it shares with many another the whine of low-flying military aircraft, now so common they no longer startle the sheep.

Happily, Bowland has also retained much of its old charm. It is still quite easy to walk for an hour or two without meeting another person.

WILDLIFE

Charles Waterton (1782-1865), naturalist and pioneer conservationist, spent his schooldays at Stonyhurst in the Ribble Valley. He left the college a portrait of himself and his collection of stuffed birds and beasts collected in many parts of the world.

In Bowland today are animal species which evolved in distant places. Sika deer, introduced to Bowland about 1906 for sport, are descended from deer which evolved on islands in the Japanese archipelago.

The pheasant, which is reared for sport, is a descendant of ancient jungle fowl living in the East. Canada geese, now in a flock 400 strong at Stocks Reservoir, hail – as the name implies – from the New World. The grey squirrel scavenging for food beneath a Bowland oak or scuttering up the smooth trunk of a beech is another introduction from North America, while feral mink are descended from escapees at Lancashire fur farms.

Some typical bird habitats:

Moorland and crags The image of a hen harrier is a wayside logo of the Forest of Bowland. In the 1960s, birdwatchers had to be content with a glimpse of a wintering harrier in the vicinity of Stocks Reservoir (*walk 9*). Then came the news of harriers nesting on the Bowland moors. The location of any nests is not publicly revealed.

A harrier – slim, lively, and long-tailed – may be seen in low-gliding flight, the long, narrow wings being held in a shallow V-shape. This predator snatches its prey with its talons. The display flight in spring is exuberant, and the bird climbs, rolls and dives as though through the sheer joy of living. It has a chattering call, varying in pitch.

The cock bird is most readily identified, having an ash-grey upper plumage which stands out from the dun colours of the landscape. The rump is white, and the trailing edges and tips of the wings are black. The female harrier is dark brown. The nest is on the ground.

The peregrine falcon maintains a tenuous hold on Bowland. Red eggs are laid in a depression on a cragside ledge. The birds cut through the air cleanly on scimitar-shaped wings, and attain an impressive speed when 'stooping' on winged prey such as pigeons.

The merlin, smallest of our falcons, sweeps a tract of moorland in a light and erratic way before fixing its attention and capturing some luckless pipit or lark. Merlins nest among the heather. The male bird is slate-blue above; the female is brownish.

The district has few sheer cliffs, so old quarries are important nesting places, with kestrel, little owl, jackdaw and stock dove taking advantage of ledges or crannies.

Bowland has some outstanding grouse moors, rich in ling and berried plants like bilberry. Here the red grouse are more numerous and lively than on more celebrated moors in Scotland. On Tarnbrook Fell, the grouse share their moorland nesting grounds with hundreds of pairs of lesser black-backed and herring gulls (*walk 3*).

Controlled burning of the rank heather in March provides new growth to sustain the grouse and moorland sheep. If well done, in strips, the swiddening (burning) leads to a moor with heather at various ages.

The red grouse is a localised form of the willow grouse of North America and Scandinavia. The cock bird has a shiny, reddish-brown plumage and red eye-wattles. The hen bird is less conspicuous, especially in springtime, when she has a cryptic colouration that is almost yellow, darkly barred, and sits like a feathered tea-cosy, swaddling her eggs or brooding her chicks.

A dependence on heather for food makes

the grouse a virtual prisoner on the moors, from which the birds move only if forced to do so in times of thick snow. Dispirited grouse are then seen perched on walls around farms and villages. Many of the best moors have no public access but, in Bowland, secondary roads run near some of them and in early spring the grouse may be observed using the car as a 'hide'.

The red grouse, carrion crow and the diminutive wren of the high crags are virtually the only species of bird on the moors in midwinter.

Bowland's high ground includes large tracts of mossland which is attractive to waders like the golden plover and dunlin. A golden plover, with dark brown underparts and dark mantle flecked with gold, is of the southern race, much lighter in tone than the bird which nests in Iceland and other points north.

The dunlin (the so-called 'plover's page') has a chestnut colouration, with black streaks on the head and upper parts, and black on the lower breast. The preferred nesting area is on moorland where there is standing water. Bowland birds may be seen feeding by Stocks Reservoir (*walk 9*).

Sometimes, in early May, a small 'trip' of dotterel is seen on traditional hilltop haunts while in passage between wintering grounds by the Mediterranean to their breeding places on northern mountains. One or two dotterel have been observed while resting and feeding

Red grouse feed entirely on the shoots of ling. The bird is an island variant of the willow grouse, which is well-established across the northern world.

15

Meadow pipits. This species, the most common bird of rough grassland, may startle you as it flutters from its nest in a tuft of coarse vegetation.

during the southerly migration in autumn. Meanwhile, snow buntings – some of Icelandic origin – winter where the grass named mollinia is common.

Marginal land The black grouse is a species of 'white' (grassy) land. The numbers have declined greatly. Old lekking (display) grounds in the upper Hodder Valley are now smothered in conifer trees. In severe winter weather, birds may be seen stripping thorn trees of their berries in the upper dales.

The carrion crow, which nests on some of the solitary fellside trees, is more numerous and less shy than it was now that gamekeepers are comparatively few in number.

By about mid-March, small birds like skylarks and meadow pipits are in their

nesting areas. A skylark, rising like a feathered helicopter until it is only a speck against the blue, enlivens many tracts of rough ground with its sweet song.

The meadow pipit is a relatively common bird. In its display flight the bird resembles a shuttlecock, its wing and tail feathers being held stiffly outwards. The pipit draws attention to itself by its song as it slowly descends to earth. The nest, of particularly neat construction, lies deep in a tuft of herbage. Sometimes, you are not aware of it until, at a range of a few feet, you see a pipit spring up almost at your feet.

The whinchat, a somewhat stocky bird with a white stripe over each eye, clicks and 'churs' while perched on a low bush or shrub in its favourite wasteland areas, the scraggy edges of moors where bracken and coarse grasses grow. The sparrowhawks of Gisburn Forest (*walk 10*) have the whinchat on their menu.

Afforestation of marginal ground which once supported a smattering of small hill farms gave the barn owls a chance, for they took advantage of the deserted buildings. A hissing sound from the young stimulated the adult birds to go hunting, and those in Gisburn Forest flew sorties both over open ground and along the forest 'rides'.

However, over more recent years, the buildings have been steadily demolished and, as a result, the barn owl population has been significantly reduced. Similarly, a pair of kestrels which once nested in a hole in the bedroom of what had been a farmhouse and starlings which reared their young in out-buildings have been forced to find alternative accommodation.

Damp pastures were known to old-time Bowland farmers as 'tewit-grund', after the lapwing, which needs boggy areas as feeding places for its chicks. The lapwing has a spiky head crest which is especially long in the male. The mantle is of iridescent greenish-black and the bird has white underparts with chestnut under the tail-coverts.

The lapwing draws attention to itself in spring by its reedy calls and an acrobatic display flight. If you go too near a nest, the cock bird dives, beating its broad black-tipped wings in such a way they produce a droning sound.

Snipe and redshank, birds of marginal land, are less common than they were. The redshank is well named. See it perched on the capstone of a wall and it shows off its long orange-red legs. When the redshank's suspicions have been aroused, an intruder is greeted to a noisy round of alarm calls.

Conifer plantations Large tracts of conifer are a relatively new type of habitat. In the early days of planting, the area teems with voles and attracts predators like short-eared owls. In the maturing forest, the goldcrest hangs its hammock-like nest from the branch of a spruce tree.

Starlings, which nest widely in Bowland, concentrate on some conifered areas in winter, and here they roost in vast numbers, augmented by Continental starlings, bird refugees from a harsher climate. As the short winter day draws to a close, large groups of starlings arrive at selected areas and put on an impressive pre-roosting display of massed aerobatics.

The European population of starlings has declined but, at its peak some years ago, a roost of wintering starlings in trees at Beacon Hill near Chipping was estimated to hold a maximum of two million birds. Another large roost was found in a conifer plantation on Grindleton Fell.

The starlings packed together for warmth and by their copious droppings polluted and killed many trees. Of almost 6,000 birds captured and ringed at Beacon Hill in the 1960s, 97 were recovered, 40 on the Continent, eastwards into Russia.

Long-eared owls sometimes nest where there are copses of Scots pines. Sparrow-hawks are fond of larch plantations and usually nest at an elevation of about 12 ft (3½m). The goshawk has been reported from the Ribble Valley. The tawny owl is relatively common: the *kewick* sound is made by the female; the male is the hooter.

The siskin, a bird with a bright yellow plumage and a crossbill with twisted mandibles, has been seen in Gisburn Forest east of Stocks Reservoir (*walk 10*), though much clear-felling has taken place here. The coniferous forest attracts redpolls and titmice, especially the cole tit. The wood pigeon finds much cover here.

Fieldfares and redwings, which are immigrant thrushes, escaping the rigours of winter in northern Europe and Scandinavia, roost in separate conifered areas.

Broadleaf woodland On the gathering grounds of Stocks Reservoir, in the upper Hodder Valley, is mixed woodland. The predominant species of tree are conifers, but broadleaf trees flourish beside Bottoms Beck (*walk 9*). There is, therefore, a wider range of birds than if the whole area grew conifers. In a purely deciduous wood – including the cloughs – where many trees are quite old, a typical species is the redstart.

Woodland birds include the chaffinch, chiffchaff and willow warbler, from the second week of April onwards. The pied flycatcher has been reported from woodland near Whitewell (*walk 11*). The green wood-pecker uses a dead tree as a sounding board, and drills its nesting hole with a beak also used for collecting grubs and ants. A screeching sound may either be a magpie, now very common, or a fellow member of the crow family – the jay.

The nightjar used to nest in woodland glades and might do so now. Another ground-nester is the woodcock, which is plump, with a long bill and a cryptic colour-ation. This enables it to blend perfectly with the woodland litter. The cock woodcock has a special flight, known as 'roding', which is undertaken at dusk. A bird flies with slow-beating wings at a height of about 50 feet (15m) and periodically utters sounds which have been described as 'three grunts and a squeak'.

Rough pastureland The short-eared owl, a long-winged hunter by day, may return to its Bowland haunts as early as February. The display flight of the cock bird includes wing-claps beneath its body, which look spectacular and can be heard for a considerable distance. This diurnal owl patrols the rough pastures on its quest for food. The field vole is a common prey and – if it is abundant – the short-eared owls will rear a large number of young. The little owl, with a flattened top to

its head, may be seen perched on trees or disused buildings.

Skeins of geese of Icelandic origin – mainly pinkfooted geese – are observed in winter, as birds head for the Ribble Estuary or Martin Mere. Most sightings are in December and January, though the birds arrive as early as mid-September.

Reservoirs and rivers Canada geese are numerous at Stocks Reservoir in the upper Hodder (*walk 9*), where a visitor in winter might count up to 400 birds. Pairs nest on high ground and walk their young to the reservoir. The Canada goose is large, with a black head and neck, white cheeks and 'chinstrap'.

Most geese like wide open spaces, but the Canada goose evolved in a semi-forested area of North America. When introduced to England as a domesticated bird, the Canada goose was used for decorative purposes in the grounds of large houses. The numbers grew in the eighteenth century and, by the mid-nineteenth century, feral flocks were known.

The Canada goose was well-established in the North of England by the 1890s and is now very common in places. The Hodder Valley birds are happy in their partly-wooded area. Many northern birds have a moult migration in summer to Beauly Firth, just north of Inverness in Scotland.

Among the ornithological surprises at Stocks Reservoir are the presence of a solitary barnacle goose and four bluephase snow geese, of a species which nest in north-west Greenland and adjacent parts of Canada. These strangers are probably escapees from a waterfowl collection.

A pair of little owls on their first excursion from the nesting hole. Their ideal habitat is open fields and hedgerows.

18

At Stocks, the osprey is an occasional passage migrant, and so are black terns, seen in spring. The island in Stocks becomes congested with nesting black-headed gulls.

Many species of duck – mallard, tufted, merganser, goosander, wigeon, goldeneye – turn up in winter. The goldeneye is a readily-identified species because of the circlet of white on its head, and wigeon are epecially numerous towards the end of winter.

Brooks and becks hold dippers, grey wagtails and sandpipers. The main rivers, sheltered in their snug valleys from the worst of the weather, have kingfishers, where good supplies of minnows are found.

Pairs of oystercatchers nest on shingle banks. The oystercatcher, a large, brash, pied bird with orange-red beak and flesh-pink legs, stands out against the Bowland greens. Some pairs of this coastal species began to nest inland and were reported by the Ribble in the 1950s. Now it is also found nesting in fields. The call of an oystercatcher – a strident *kleep* – draws attention to the bird.

Goosander and red-breasted merganser now nest in the Ribble Valley; there are also wintering birds at Stocks Reservoir.

Grassland At home on marginal ground, pasture or meadow, the curlew makes its presence felt from March until the end of August. The bird is familiar to countrygoers, being lanky, streaky-brown and with a long curved bill. In spring, the curlew glides above the nesting area uttering the familiar bubbling trill. The curved bill is ideal for probing for food in the damp ground of Bowland. Alas, many half-grown chicks in the meadows are killed by machines being used to take the second cut of grass for silage.

Widespread throughout Bowland, from lowland farms to gills penetrating the moors, are good stocks of pheasant – either hand-reared poults or feral birds which have reverted to the wild.

Another notable game-bird, the partridge, may still be seen, but in smaller numbers than hitherto because the drainage, ploughing and re-seeding of many lowland fields has diminished the food supply. Nowadays, partridge thrive best on marginal land. Even so, you may see a family party dust-bathing beside a lowland road.

Roadsides The kestrel hovers over the verges of major roads. When a deep rock-cutting was made through limestone at Chatburn as part of the Clitheroe bypass, jackdaws began nesting on one of the faces.

In early autumn, chaffinches are seen on those stretches of road where beech mast has fallen and has been shattered by passing traffic, exposing the seeds.

Barn owls, of a species which is becoming rare in England, have a dangerous habit of flying low over roads.

Towns and villages In about 1980, the collared dove (which had arrived in England during a vigorous extension of its range in the early 1950s) was nesting at Clitheroe. It is now a relatively common bird.

Mammals The Forest of Bowland, with its bountiful timber, its deer, wild swine and wild cattle, was under pressure from agriculture even during the Middle Ages. The White Bull Inn at Gisburn alludes to the white cattle kept on the 100 acres (40ha) of Gisburne (*sic*) Park until 1859. A story relates that their ancestors roamed the forest and at the dissolution they were conveyed there from the monastic park at Whalley – lured by music, presumably a flautist.

The last of the indigenous deer, red and fallow, were slaughtered about 1805, but almost a century later, Peter Ormerod of Wyresdale and Lord Ribblesdale of Gisburne Park, were hunting with imported black fallow, followed by a more 'sporty' deer species, the sika, which has an Asian origin. (Sika had been introduced to Powerscourt, just south of Dublin, in about 1860, and surplus animals were available to English landowners.)

Introduced in the first decade of this century, to be hunted by the Ribblesdale Buckhounds, the deer were not popular with landowners because of damage caused to trees. Peter Ormerod occasionally arrived at the home of an aggrieved squire with a bundle of young trees as compensation. One man, noting the pathetically small number of saplings, retorted: 'Some people can be bribed and I'm one of them – but not with tuppence'.

From the initial stock the number of sika deer built up slowly until they were able, through afforestation with conifers, to spread into the upper Hodder.

Sika are medium-sized deer, with a summer coat of dappled chestnut and wearing a thicker winter coat of grey-brown. The stag carries simple branched antlers which are cast in spring. New growth is complete by August, in time for the autumnal rut (mating season). The deer lie up in small woods or wooded gills, and graze in fields which have been ploughed and re-seeded, so providing lush food.

A sika's alarm call is a short, sharp scream, rather like a whistle. In the rut, a stag in the presence of hinds has a variety of calls, notably (and mainly at dusk) a sequence of three or four squeals which, from a distance, sound like sweet whistles.

In recent times, roe deer spreading from the Lune Valley up the valley of the Wenning, thence to the gills around Keasden, found in the new coniferous tract on the watershed of Stocks reservoir two basic requirements – sanctuary and good feeding. Roe, which is a relatively small deer and with the buck carrying small antlers, are now found in most parts of Bowland and the Ribble Valley. The caudal disc, in contrast to that of the sika, is kidney-shaped and prominently white. The alarm call of a roe buck is a gruff bark.

Badgers have their setts (burrows) in quiet woodland and gills. Where they are not disturbed by humans, they emerge in the last hour of daylight. Spring, when a sow badger has her cubs in attendance, is a particularly good time to watch them. Badgers, which are hygenic animals, regularly bring out old bedding and take down more bracken to replace it. The red fox is quite common, though rarely seen in daylight unless disturbed. The dog fox barks at night in late January or early February, making his presence known during the mating season.

The brown hare is distinguished from the rabbit by its larger size and the black tips to the long ears. The hare has a form (lying place among vegetation) which is not hard to find if the animal has been flushed at close quarters. Rest your palm on the form and you will find it is still warm from the hare's body. Leverets (young hares) are born in spring. Some are killed by farm machinery.

Grey squirrels, descendants of animals which were introduced from North America in 1876, have swept through areas where once the red squirrel was found. It may be that when the population of red squirrels is low as part of its natural population cycle, the grey finds it easy to move into a new area, where it annoys the forester by stripping bark from trees to feed on the underlying material.

The short-tailed or field vole, a staple food for owls and hawks, periodically increases its numbers to almost plague proportions ('vole years') and permits a species like the short-eared owl to thrive. Vole tunnels through grass are particularly evident as the snow thaws from open ground in afforested areas and where there is rank (dense) vegetation elsewhere.

Fish Two migratory fish – salmon and sea trout – follow the Ribble and Hodder and its tributary becks to spawn in the headwaters. The rivers authority maintains a hatchery in

A sika stag, in summer coat and in the process of growing new antlers.

Bowland to augment the stock of both species in the two main rivers.

The Bowland rivers used to have an outstanding spring run of salmon. From one good pool, on three successive days in the early sixteenth century, a man lifted out 1,000, 600 and 200 fish respectively.

Sea trout are running in June if there is a good water, and they follow both the main rivers and some of the becks. Their movement up the river is usually indicated by the presence of mergansers and cormorants, the latter species being most often seen on the Ribchester reach of the Ribble. A few cormorants operate in the Hodder Valley.

Differences in appearance are noted between the salmon in the Ribble and those in the Hodder. Hodder salmon grow more slowly than those in the neighbouring watercourse, and they are noticeably deeper in the shoulder than their Ribble cousins. Whereas the Ribble fish spawn in November, those following the Hodder spawn in December.

Salmon spend their early lives in fresh water and then migrate as 'smolts' (young river fish) to the deep water off Greenland to feed up, returning in about three years to their native rivers to breed, the hen fish to deposit eggs, the cock fish (which has a hooked lower jaw at this time) fertilising them with its 'milt' or sperm.

The best watercourses are those fed by springs or flowing over limestone, as compared with brooks which take much of their water from afforested ground, where the run-off is acidic.

Brown trout are found in most Bowland waters, including Stocks Reservoir, the southern end of which has been opened up to anglers, who fish for brown and rainbow trout (*walk 9*). Permits for the reservoir are available from the fisherman's cabin at Stocks (tel: 020066 602).

Many brooks carry bullheads and stone loach. Eels are less numerous than they were but elvers, which are small and with an appearance similar to bootlaces, move into fresh water in the spring, having been borne to our shores by the Gulf Stream. Their breeding routine is just the opposite of the salmon. The eels feed up in fresh water and then migrate to salt water for breeding.

Butterflies and moths Moorland tracts, where ling intermingles with bilberry, have some good colonies of the green hairstreak butterfly, and the adults are on the wing in May and June. The undersides of the wings are a brilliant green, which tones with the leaves.

The meadow brown, which feeds on various grasses, is relatively common. Towards the end of July, six-spot burnets are seen on vetch. A hatch of small tortoise-shell butterflies brings life and colour to a normally drab nettle-bed beside a ruined building or wall.

Emperor moths are common locally, the larvae being found on heather. Willowherb is the main food plant of the caterpillars of the elephant hawk moth, which is pink and light brown in tone. The association with an elephant is from the supposed resemblance to an elephant's head which, if threatened, the caterpillar retracts into its body.

The fox moth has an association with bilberry. Above the heather moors in August the northern eggar moth takes flight.

FLORA

Forest and woodland Within historical times, most of the Bowland area was well-timbered. Trees were to be found up to 1,600 feet (488m) above sea level, as the condition of the soil and underlying rock dictated.

In those early ages, a widespread species of tree was the sessile oak (the acorns are sessile, which means 'stalkless'), in the company of ash, hazel, holly and probably wych elm. In the damper places, such as by rivers, the alder flourished.

The name 'Forest of Bowland' must not be taken to imply that in Norman times virtually all the area was under timber. As mentioned, *foras* was land set apart as a game preserve for the benefit of the king and nobility. At an early date, inroads were being made as land was cleared for farming and by their browsing the domestic animals prevented any natural regeneration.

In 1503, most of the Bowland pastures were being leased by Sir Edward Stanley, the timber including old hollins, old heythornes, old hassilles, old crabtrees and oller wood – or, using modern names, holly, hawthorn, hazel, crab and alder.

A range of typical Bowland vegetation is to be found at Beacon Fell Country Park, where trees, grasses and heathers now grow un-checked by grazing animals.

If you seek 'relict' areas of the former woodland cover, look in some of the dry cloughs, where there was difficulty of access and thus of farm management. Here grow sessile oak, downy birch, rowan and perhaps holly.

Where the clough woodland is moist, such as from ground water, ash may be dominant, having the company of alder, hazel and, possibly, the shrub known as bird cherry.

Old, often gnarled trees stand around old fields, testifying to the woodland days. Haw-thorn is the most common hedgerow tree, planted to deter footloose stock. Its rate of growth was so impressive that it was also called 'quickthorn'. The fruit, known as haws, takes on a dark red shade in early autumn. Blackthorn sports white flowers in spring. The fruit, known as sloes, is the basis of sloe gin.

The sycamore, which may have been intro-duced to Britain by the Romans, is commonly seen in the deciduous woodland beside the rivers Hodder and Ribble. Sycamore flowers appear in May or June. In October, a breeze sends the winged seeds twirling through the air, each revolving like the blades of a tiny helicopter. In the Ribble Valley, wild cherry adorns some of the woods.

Where land was developed as part of large private estates, the eighteenth-century fashion was for woods composed of beech and ash. Later, stands of Scots pine were popular.

Local authorities planted conifers on the gathering grounds of reservoirs. The sitka spruce, which is now common, was intro-duced into this country from north-west America in 1831 and thrives in an area of high rainfall.

Bowland, having much clay and impeded drainage, does not perfectly suit the sitka spruce which, unless the water table has been lowered by deep ploughing, puts out a shallow rooting system. At an age of about twenty years, a plantation is vulnerable to 'wind-blow'.

The water authorities planted both deci-duous and coniferous trees. In the Black Moss area south of Pendle, North West Water has ninety-one acres (37ha) of forest, a development of a planting scheme inaugur-ated in 1900, when Slacks Wood was planted with beech and sycamore. Soon, the Nelson Waterworks were engaged in afforestation with conifers.

In 1901, part of Whitehough Forest was planted with sycamores, and in 1933 this stock of growing timber was augmented by both sycamore and sitka spruce. Aitken Wood (46 acres/19ha), planted in 1935, contains some Scots pine.

The conifers of other estate plantings, and those brought in by the Forestry Commission, frequently have an under-storey of holly, which once was a major forest tree. The pines, spruces and firs are of New World origin. The commonest introduction to Bowland is the sitka spruce.

Bowland Forest, of the Forestry Commission, consists of about twenty-five scattered woods. The large afforested area lying to the east of Stocks Reservoir, and another tract, on Grindleton Fell, are predominantly of

Beech leaves and mast. The mast is a nutritious food for mammals and, in old forest days, fattened up a large number of domestic pigs.

Fly agaric – a favourite perch for pixies and elves in children's books, but in reality a highly poisonous member of the fungi family.

conifer trees. They blot out the scene, and, even when brashed (thinned out), have a depressingly dark appearance.

Apart from sitka spruce, the new forests hold Lodgepole pine, Norway spruce, Scots pine and larch, which casts its needles in autumn and, in spring, gives the forest a brilliantly green hue with the brightness of its new foliage.

Where broadleaved woodland occurs, this is often for amenity – to break up the rigid lines of the plantations.

The flora of an area is closely related to the geology. Over much of Bowland, the rocks give rise to acid soils. An exception is in Little Bowland and the Clitheroe area, where limestone obtrudes. Even so, the boulder clay associated with the melting of glacial ice

masks much of the limestone, nullifying its effects. In Bowland, boulder clay extends to an elevation of some 600 feet (183m).

Moorland The Bowland 'tops' are mostly covered by blanket bog, creating an acidic environment. A mosaic of plant species includes heather, bilberry, cowberry and crowberry. The Bowland fells have the largest area of continuous heather moorland in Lancashire.

Cloudberry, an arctic species which in Bowland is close to the southern extent of its range, roots in peat and produces a stem supporting a single white flower and a leaf which is like a miniature sycamore. The fruit of the cloudberry has been described as resembling an amber raspberry.

Where moorland is carefully managed for grouse, a profusion of heather is found. In areas over-grazed by sheep, the heather shoots are eaten in preference to the coarse grasses and in due course the moorland has degenerated into a sedge moor, the sedge in question being cotton-grass.

On the Bowland blanket bog, the hare's tail cotton-grass (which has a single fluffy head) is most common. The plant creates tussocks which impede the walker. The common cotton-grass (with multiple flowering heads) grows more commonly in marshy areas.

Moorsides In boggy areas, purple moor-grass forms tussocks in areas of poor management. Water seeping from the ground, and producing an acid flush, is ideal for such plants as bog asphodel and sundew (an insectiverous plant). Acidic grassland also suits heath bedstraw, tormentil (with its four neat yellow petals) and marsh violet (its blunt petals lilac in shade).

Bracken occurs on many Bowland fells and is usually a sign of over-grazing. At one time, Bowland farmers mowed bracken in autumn and used it as bedding for the in-wintering stock, but this no longer occurs. Spraying of bracken from the air has to be maintained for several years for the effect to be worthwhile.

Of specialist interest is chickweed winter-green, a rare plant found on the edge of one tract of moorland, in an area which once was woodland. A specimen of lesser twayblade, reported from an upland flush in the early

The colour of bracken changes with the seasons, from bright to dark green, thence to the coppery reds and golds of autumn. In living memory, bracken has swamped large tracts of upland grazing land.

1970s, was the first record in Lancashire for many years.

Cloughs and woodland   The plantlife of the cloughs, those V-shaped fellside valleys which were ignored as being impractical to farm, represent a relic of the former woodland flora. Ancient woodland is that which has not been clear-felled or has been essentially woodland for centuries.

Examples of semi-natural woodland occur alongside the main rivers, the Hodder and Ribble.

The species include wood sorrel, with its white, lilac-veined leaves, bluebell and bramble. Ferns include the broad buckler. Clumps of wavy hair-grass, which is dark green with fine leaves, may cover a large area.

Where a clough has a seepage of water from a spring, the flora includes wood anemone, with its star-like white flowers, and lesser celandine, the petals of which are narrow, glossy and yellow in hue. Water avens is characterised by its dropping flower heads. Here, too, grow golden saxifrage, bugle, ramson (wild garlic) and dog's mercury.

A seepage of water from springs in the underlying limestone stimulates the growth of primrose, dog violet, wild strawberry and moschatel (a tiny plant with five flowers forming a cube at the top of the stem). The early purple orchid is a plant of limey areas.

The wood ragwort, a plant which grows up to a height of five feet (1½m), and evolved in damp areas of the lower Alps, was introduced to the grounds of a house at Holden many years ago and has since spread, mainly along hedgerows, as far as Clitheroe and Stocks.

Conifer forests   Large areas of conifers, such as you will see by the upper Hodder and in Whitendale, are a relatively new landscape feature. In the early stages of afforestation, the rides (aisles) between plantations hold an abundance of flowers and grasses.

In cleared areas where re-planting has taken place, and particularly where areas have been fired, as in the disposal of small stuff after clear-felling, the 'fireweed' (rosebay willow herb) grows profusely and foxgloves are numerous.

Burdock, with its large, hairy seed-cases, which stick to any creature or thing with which they come in contact, may grow several feet tall.

Hedgerows and walls   Hedges are formed mainly of hawthorn, with blackthorn, holly, hazel, elder and, in the Clitheroe area of the Ribble Valley and also the valley of the Hodder, some field maple.

Limestone walls often have an abundance of mosses and some ephemeral plants such as rue-leaved saxifrage and spring whitlow-grass. In various parts of Bowland and the Ribble Valley may be seen the pinky-mauve or white flowers of fairy foxglove, an alpine plant which is typically of rocks and screes in the Alps but, introduced to English gardens, escaped from those in Bowland.

Woodland plants – celandine, wood anemone, bluebell, and lords and ladies – feature in many hedges. Early in the growing season, cow parsley and sweet cicely, with their many flowers packed on heads which have a few branches, give a frothy white appearance to the roadsides. Crush a leaf from sweet cicely and you will smell aniseed. This plant was once used for flavouring food. The greater bell-flower is a conspicuous hedgerow plant.

Meadow cranesbill flowers from June to September where there is dry grassland on a limey soil. Also look out for meadowsweet and greater burnet saxifrage.

In upland areas, such as that between Bolton-by-Bowland and Stocks Reservoir, hedge banks are often adorned by a flora which reflects the type found in meadows before agricultural improvements took place. Among the species represented are marsh

The blackthorn's white blossom appears in March; by the end of October it hangs heavy with a mass of black sloes.

marigold (also known as kingcup, and present in Britain since before the last Ice Age), water avens, bistort and meadowsweet.

The melancholy thistle (once used as a cure for melancholia) occurs locally in hedgerows. Some hedge banks sustain the dusky cranesbill, which is an escapee from gardens.

Grassland A meadow can be thought of as land on which grass is cut for hay or silage and is grazed outside the growing season, and pasture as land which is grazed the year round.

Most of the Bowland grassland is highlying and has been 'improved' by ploughing, re-seeding with a ryegrass mix, and given regular doses of chemical fertilisers and slurry (the latter being waste material from cattle in liquid form). Only a few traditional hay meadows, which were managed by the application of cattle dung and a periodic liming, remain. Some examples of these survivors are to be found in the Slaidburn area.

Hay-meadow flora appears to have evolved from that of the type of woodland which previously occupied the area. Hence the presence of bluebells and wood anemones, presumably taking their shade from the clouds. Traditional hay meadows also hold greater burnet, knapweed, ribwort plantain, yellow rattle, buttercups (meadow, creeping and bulbous), birdsfoot trefoil and red clover. Here, too, are the aromatic sweet vernal-grass and quaking grass.

In a few meadows flushed with water from underlying limestone, you might hope to see the bird's eye primrose, globe-flower and early purple orchid. Common ragwort, which is more typical of coastal areas, has become a weed in pastures. Moist areas may sport ragged robin and marsh marigold.

Waterside The flora may often be a continuation of the clough vegetation, the V-shaped valleys extending to the riverside. Here grow self heal and hairy willowherb.

Two conspicuous plants are that desirable native wild plant butterbur, which puts forth pinky spikes followed by rhubarb-like leaves, and the Himalayan (or Indian) balsam, now well-established on the Ribble below Edisford Bridge and also near Lower Hodder Bridge.

Also evident on riverbanks are flag (yellow iris) and reed canary-grass.

WALK 1: CLOUGHA PIKE AND HARE APPLETREE

Start: Quernmore. Alternatively (Easter-October):
                          Brow Top Farm. Grid Ref: 528 588
Distance: 5½ miles (9km), climbing 900 feet (275m).
OS Map: Pathfinder 659. SD 45/55
Walking Time: 3½ hours

Walk yourself into condition by 'bagging' Clougha Pike (pronounce it 'Cloffa'). At 1,355 feet (413m) it is one of the lesser fells of Bowland but when you reach the scattered boulders at its head, you will feel elated. Good weather views take in the Three Peaks, Lakeland Fells, Lancashire plain and seaboard. Choose a clear day in late July or August for preference. Then the bonny heather is blooming between the jumbled boulders of Clougha Pike. A purple carpet of heather lies along the ridge between here and Grit Fell.

Parking space at Quernmore – pronounced 'Quarmer' – is limited, but car parks exist off a minor road branching from Rigg Lane. Brow Top Craft Centre, on Quernmore Brow, has private parking and permission may be obtained to leave the car here. Brow Top also has a good cafe.

Quernmore was well-known to the Romans, who had pottery kilns in what is now the park. Some tiles were stamped as being produced by the Ala Sebosiana, a unit which in the third century AD had their main quarters in Lancaster.

From Quernmore, walk eastwards to the adjacent farms of Rowton Brook and Rooten Brook. (Those parking at Brow Foot use a connecting footpath to the farms.) At Rooten Brook, where the footpaths merge, the route to Clougha is indicated by a noticeboard attached to the side of a modern farm building.

A gate gives access to a track which soon settles down as a not-too-arduous climb to the Clougha Access Area. *En route* are three gates, each set in a drystone wall, fashioned of random pieces of dark gritstone. Notice how the waller has crossed all joints and put in plenty of through-stones for stability. The wallheads (where a wall ends) are neat and firm.

Rowton Brook is a watercourse shielded for much of its length by trees and rhododendrons, the latter descended from stock introduced into England from Asia Minor over 200 years ago, augmented by the introduction of various types. Originally planted in the grounds of big houses, the rhododendron, forming a thick shrub layer, provided cover for game such as pheasants. *Ponticum*, the species which produces purple flowers in May and June, is a menace to a landscape by its lusty colonisation of new ground.

Having passed through the gate near where the access area notice is displayed, enter a tract of moorland covered mainly by coarse grasses and rush-bobs. Too many sheep have prevented the natural regeneration of timber and so the moor is treeless now.

In the damp places are cotton-grass and sphagnum, important in the formation of peat, which occurs where plant material does not rot normally in an acid, waterlogged environment. Deposits of peat contain evidence of the old woodland conditions in the form of pieces of birch or oak.

Sphagnum grows densely in bogs, giving an illusion of firm ground. This moss is so absorbent that it retains water like a sponge. Sphagnum was gathered, dried and used as field dressings in the 1914-18 war.

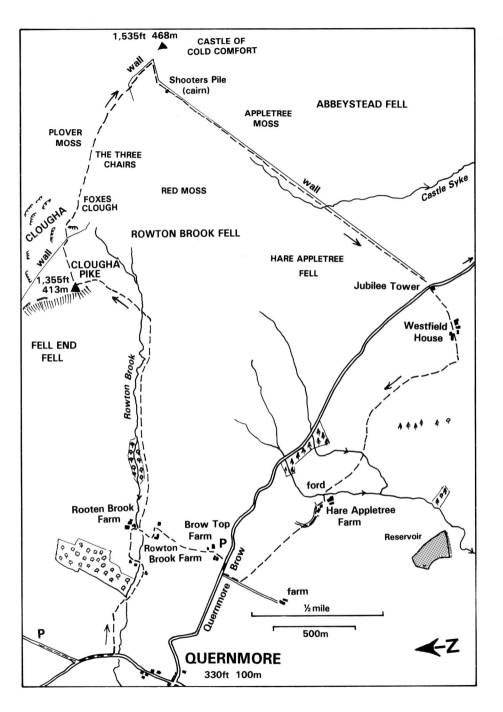

A slate-sided farmhouse beside a footpath leading to Clougha Pike.

As Clougha Pike draws near, sheep-cropped heather and closely-matted bilberry occupy the spaces between the jumble of gritstone boulders, some of which have been leached of their minerals until they are almost bone-white.

The final approach is a diagonal path, with mainly stone underfoot and a veritable rock garden of moorland plants to the right. On reaching the summit of Clougha, you will see a windbreak thrown up from loose stones. Here, too, is a trig point, now just a curiosity in an age when mapping takes place from satellites. A large cairn adorns the hill. Some rusting objects are remains of the uprights of

an iron-and-wire fence, the sort favoured by old estates to delineate their boundaries.

The map gives a scattering of names, including Plover Moss and stones known as the Three Chairs. The path extending eastwards towards Grit Fell has been well-defined by booted feet. The path goes by a small tarn, from which dragonflies take to the wing in summer.

A simple step stile leads over a post-and-wire fence, which effectively controls grazing by sheep. Notice the sudden transformation of the moorland from heather-and-bilberry to bilberry alone.

The red grouse you should see and hear

(the call is a harsh croaking) is a species peculiar to Britain, evolving as an island sub-species of the willow grouse. This bird is a specialist feeder on heather, plus such moor-land plants as bilberry and crowberry. A cock bird, which stays out of sight among the heather for most of the time, is noisy and demonstrative in spring, flying into the air and then descending with fast-beating wings and tail widespread. As the grouse descends, it utters its croaky call.

At the next fence, do not cross the stile; simply turn right and walk down the hill with the fence on your left, passing the Shooters Pile, which is a large, neat cairn. The route is now downhill to the Jubilee Tower, which was constructed in honour of Queen Victoria by James Harrison of Hare Appletree.

The view takes in the Lancashire plain and seaboard, with Blackpool Tower visible in clear conditions. You may wish to climb the tower by the stone steps but an equally good view is possible from ground level.

Use the tarmac path to Westfield House, in preference to pushing through a mini-jungle of rushes. Beyond the farm, the concrete road swings to the left; you will go to the right, using a stone stile as access to fields which stretch away to Hare Appletree. At the corner of a field where a gate is prominent, ignore it in favour of an incon-spicuous stile on the wall ahead. Climb over and head for the hamlet which is now in clear view. Some of the stiles are rickety.

A ford is negotiated to enter the hamlet, the home of farmers who may be attending to their stock. (On my last visit they were dipping sheep.)

Now follow the road for about 200 yards (180m) to a metal gate painted red. Pass through the gate to walk beside a row of old thorn trees, the trunks of which are so smooth they must have been used as rubbing posts by many generations of farm animals. A stile gives access to a concrete road, a right turn leading to Quernmore Brow, close to Brow Top.

The straggling village of Quernmore is not far off down the hill.

WALK 2: FOREST OF MEWITH AND THE GREAT STONE

Start: Bentham Bridge. Grid Ref: 668 687
Distance: 5½ miles (9km)
OS Maps: Pathfinder 650 (SD 66/76)
Walking Time: 3½ hours

The Forest of Mewith is quite well wooded, with a 'mix' of indigenous species – oak, ash, hazel, rowan and birch. Trees line the side of the River Wenning and its tributary becks. The walk goes along the fringes of Burnmoor to the Great Stone, a boulder shifted to its present position by glacial ice. So large is the stone that steps have been cut in its sides. For this outing, be well-shod and carry waterproof clothing. You are advised to park in High Bentham rather than try to find a spot to the south of the river bridge.

The walk begins on a winding road hemmed in by trees. In about 200 yards (180m), at a sign indicating Mewith Lane, take to the fields on the way to Staggarths, a pleasant farm with facilities for caravanners.

The Wenning is a little-known river outside its home area. As with most other tree-shaded watercourses, it has gathered about itself some butterbur, also known because of its large distinctive leaves as 'wild rhubarb'. The leaves develop after the flowers have died and were used to wrap up butter in the days when it was a product of nearly every local farm.

A heron at the water's edge is like a wizened post. This post has black eye-stripes. The bird unfurls its long neck as it stalks fish. Disturb it, and it will take flight, bending the neck, drawing in the head and trailing its legs behind as it gains height. The flight call of a heron is a loud *frank*.

The Wenning, a tributary of the Lune, is so-named from the merger of becks near Clapham station, one of them having its nursery stretches near Bowland Knotts. Thomas Dixon, a Romantic poet of two centuries and more ago, who praised the Wenning in verse, wrote of the Keasden watercourses:

> 'From Bowland's Knotts and Burn-
>   moor's cloud-capped crown
> Two moss-stained, noisy streams come
>   foaming down.'

Salmon and sea trout use redds (gravel beds used for spawning) in the Wenning and some of the becks. Where the Wenning performs a graceful sweep, you will see mighty Ingleborough (2,373 ft/723m) looming beyond hay meadows fringed by hedges, not walls.

In summer, you will be able to watch silage-making, using tractor-drawn machines. The old business of mowing grass to be sun- and wind-dried into hay is gone. Silage is grass taken green, after being wilted a little, and the most common way of storing it is now the black plastic bag.

Follow around the tract of woodland (on a path waymarked by yellow arrows, two of which appear side by side on one of the big trees). You may relax for a while at a wooden seat which has its back to a stretch of wall. Then move on to the derelict Dawson Close, in its sea of nettles, a plant which is often associated with places where the ground has been disturbed by settlers.

The path leads to Gill Brow Wood, where a footbridge has been installed. Rowan trees are locally numerous. In late summer, the vermilion berries are showy, some people converting them into a jelly which tradition-ally is served with game. Thrushes fall upon the berries hungrily. The mopping-up oper-ation is carried out in autumn by two immi-grant species – fieldfares and redwings,

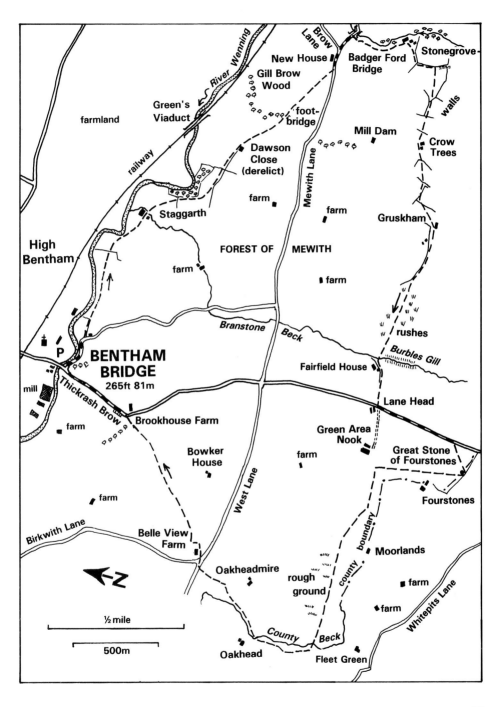

The distinctive, flat-topped profile of Ingleborough from Mewith.

refugees from the harsh winter of their native Scandinavia.

The fieldfare, a large and noisy thrush, has grey patches on its plumage. The voice is a harsh chacking sound. The redwing, which has a sweeter voice, sports a white eye-stripe. The reddy patch under the wing is seen when the bird is in flight.

The old woods have a scattering of silver birch, named after the colour of the bark. In mature trees, the trunk has some attractive, diamond-shaped black patches. The silver birch is a pioneering species and one which does not normally live to a great age, being prone to fungal attacks.

On crossing a footbridge, bear right (not left, as you might imagine from seeing a well-used track) to a stile in a wall, crossing the

land beyond to a point near New House, where you join the road until you see a sign indicating Stonegrove.

Beyond this farm, the track passes to the left of a large field. A stile in the post-and-wire fence should be used to indicate an incoming path (from the direction of Badger Ford Beck, doubtless named after the nickname for an itinerant trader).

Your route lies across the field on the way to Crow Trees. Mill Dam, a cluster of buildings, the old importance of which is indicated by a complex system of footpaths, has been used as a meeting place by Methodists for a considerable period. I have been among those who have conducted services in the front room of the farmhouse, using a rostrum slipped over the back of a chair.

The great Stone of Fourstones, an ice-borne boulder up which steps have been cut for curious visitiors. Take care if you use these steps.

When I allowed my attention to stray, I enjoyed a splendid view of Ingleborough through the window.

Continue the walk to Gruskham, with views of Burnmoor, a considerable expanse of moorland where sheep and grouse co-exist. The heather is kept young and palatable for both creatures by burning in strips towards the end of winter, the smoke from carefully-controlled moorland fires rising into the calm air, for the weather must be dry and calm for 'swiddening', as the process is known.

The lower part of Burnmoor is grassy, with rushes and some bracken, the fronds of which uncurl in spring like a bishop's crozier. Bracken spreads through underground rhizomes.

Aim initially for a left-hand group of three trees to the east. Soon, Fairfield will come into view – on the far side of steep-sided Burbles Gill, which has a footpath and a simple wooden bridge.

Now, visible on the moor, is the Great Stone of Fourstones. Little is known about this monstrous boulder beyond its glacial origin. Over the years, visitors have chiselled names and dates into the rock. Take care if you decide to ascend the Stone, for some of the steps are badly worn.

Fourstones, a large house within a walled area, is passed to the right. Join the track for Moorlands Farm, but turn off just before a gate is reached to follow a wall round to County Beck which divides Yorkshire from Lancashire.

Thence on the homeward stretch, via Oakhead, Belle View (where a footpath has been re-routed round the buildings) and, descending through fields, to Brookhouse Farm.

Thickrash Brow, a metalled way, leads you swiftly down to the starting point of the walk.

WALK 3: WARDS STONE VIA TARNBROOK

Start: Abbeystead. Grid Ref: 563 543
Distance: Over 12½ miles (20km), climbing 1,600 feet (490m)
OS Maps: Pathfinder 660 (SD 65/75) and Pathfinder 659 (SD 45/55)
Walking Time: 7½ hours

It is a long slog to Wards Stone, at 1,836 feet (560m) the highest point in Bowland, using a route which makes full use of an access area, though it may be closed periodically for grouse-shooting or if there is a high fire risk. Choose a day when there is adequate daylight. The felltops should be clear. Carry a compass and waterproof clothing. Have durable footwear, preferably boots.

Half the pleasure of this outing is in the views, especially those to the north, taking in the Lakeland Fells and Three Peaks. To the south are the Pendle and Bowland ridges. Westwards, in good weather, the sun brings a gleam to Morecambe Bay and Blackpool Tower stands, pencil-thin, beyond the Lancashire plain.

Abbeystead, where you may park the car, is a village of stylish buildings – many Victorian – set in woodland. A school was founded and endowed here in 1674. The office of the Duke of Westminster deals with an estate of 19,500 acres (6,700ha).

Head eastwards, crossing Stoops Bridge over the Tarnbrook Wyre, which soon blends its water with the Marshaw Wyre to form the River Wyre, the estuary of which is at Fleetwood. From Stoops Bridge, the road, known as Strait Lane, sets you on your way to Tarnbrook.

Where Strait Lane takes a sharp left turn, continue straight on, using a broad gate into an orchard, beyond which a step stile gives access to the fields. The woodland (right) to the north of Abbeystead House contains mature deciduous trees – sycamore, oak, some rowan, and also larch. While crossing the first large field, look northwards to take in details of the moorland ridge, of which Wards Stone is a part.

The gritstone walls are made of 'dry' stones (no mortar). Should a stretch of wall be gapped, the materials for its repair are on the spot. The path through the fields is waymarked with yellow arrows. A plethora of arrows marks a crossing of footpaths near Higher Emmetts; keep straight on, passing two ancient but not very large oak trees, and an earthen bank containing some stone, and adjacent ditch, presumably an ancient boundary, now replaced by posts and wire. The shapely, heathered hill to the south has the unwieldy name of Hawthornthwaite Fell, the domain of grouse and sheep, with no public rights of way.

The path reaches a minor road, beyond which is Top of Emmetts. Bear right just before the yard is reached and cross more fields to Tarnbrook. Waymarking is effective and, by and large, the various stiles are in good condition. Farm life includes the ensilement of meadow grass. The silage is made into huge rolls which are enveloped in black plastic (notice the orderly rows of 'big bag silage' near a farm at Tarnbrook).

This is an area of lush rye-grass and neatly-trimmed thorn hedges. The hedges of Bowland are mainly of thorn but other representative species are blackthorn, holly and even crab apple.

Meadows give way to pastures, the resort of cattle and horned sheep, the cattle having a preponderance of Friesian stock (a black and white type which originated in the Low Countries) and the sheep being mainly of the

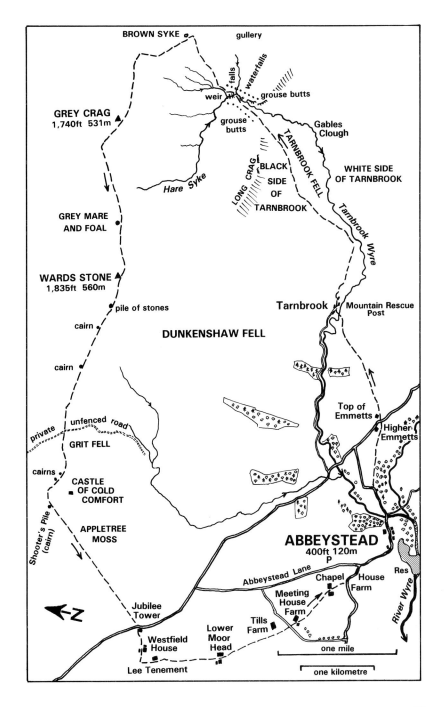

BROWN SYKE · · gullery

waterfalls

falls

weir · · grouse butts

GREY CRAG
1,740ft 531m

grouse butts

Gables Clough

TARNBROOK FELL

LONG CRAG

BLACK SIDE OF TARNBROOK

WHITE SIDE OF TARNBROOK

Hare Syke

Tarnbrook Wyre

GREY MARE AND FOAL ·

WARDS STONE ▲
1,835ft 560m

· pile of stones

cairn ·

Tarnbrook · Mountain Rescue Post

DUNKENSHAW FELL

cairn ·

Top of Emmetts

unfenced road

private

GRIT FELL

Higher Emmetts

cairns ·

CASTLE OF COLD COMFORT ■

Shooter's Pile (cairn)

APPLETREE MOSS

ABBEYSTEAD
400ft 120m
P

Res

Abbeystead Lane

Chapel ■ House Farm

←Z

Meeting House Farm

Jubilee Tower

Lower Moor Head

Tills Farm ■

River Wyre

Westfield House ■

one mile

Lee Tenement

one kilometre

39

Swaledale breed (the type for which was set by farmers living on and around Tan Hill on the high Pennines).

Greenside Hill (to the east) is well-named and, with its outbarn, drystone walls and some woodland, is a microcosm of farming in Bowland. The drystone walls include 'cripple holes', which allow for mixed grazing, the holes being sufficient only for the passage of sheep, which may graze over a wider area, the cattle being restrained by the walls.

In spring and summer, the curlews dip and call. Oystercatchers nest in the area and their presence is announced by their resounding *kleep*.

At Tarnbrook, what is marked as a 'ford' on the Pathfinder map is now a bridge.

Tarnbrook, which lies in a secluded little valley at the approach to the high fells, was once the home of twenty-five families, some of whom earned their livelihood making hats. The exposed nature of the fells beyond is indicated by the presence at Tarnbrook of a mountain rescue post. A cottage door is fringed by an old-fashioned rose named Dorothy Perkins.

A gate marked Gilberton (a farm) is where we leave the lowlands for the highlands on the Wards Stone-Tarnbrook access track, seven and a half miles (12km) long to Grit Fell, being limited to a strip of ground. There is a prohibition on dogs and fires, and you must beware of unexploded shells (!).

The track meanders amiably, between rush and coarse grass, before taking to the heights.

Moorland pines near Tarnbrook are seen by those who follow the long route to Wards Stone.

Tormentil, which grows on acid land up to around 2,000 feet (610m), is easily recognised because of its diminutive size and the four yellow petals, neatly arranged. The 'torment' of the plant's name was toothache, even colic, which the herbalists of old attempted to alleviate using a liquid from boiling the astringent roots.

The floral interest also includes bell-heather, here in a grassy setting. Bell-heather, which is prominent because it flowers ahead of the ling, and thrives on the driest parts of a moor, is, in late summer, hung with crimson-purple bells. These are much larger than the purple flowers decking the long, loose spikes of the ling. Swallows from nearby outbarns hunt insects over the edge of the moor.

To your left is the Black Side (peat) of Tarnbrook Fell and to the right, across Gables Clough, is the White Side (grassland). A fascinating aspect of the scenery is the pattern of drystone walls, forming small crofts where sheep are assembled for routine jobs like dipping and clipping. Notice also the cluster of Scots pines, giving the area a Scottish flavour.

The gradient of the track, which has a good surface and is quite capable of handling wheeled traffic, makes walking relatively easy. Eventually it peters out and you go forward on a peaty track. To the left are jumbled, weathered boulders and clumps of heather. On the right is the clough (remember to pronounce it 'cloo'), where the Tarnbrook Wyre, here in its nursery stretch, tumbles down a rocky staircase, producing two splendid falls. Wooden baulks between walls composed of large, well-trimmed stones, make a splendid dining area.

In spring and early summer, the sky seems to be half-full of wheeling, wailing gulls – medium-sized birds, both lesser black-backs and herring gulls – which nest on Tarnbrook Fell to the east. In that direction, too, is Wolfhole Crag, which is out of bounds. This is a pity. With such an evocative name and a summit composed of wind and frost-sculpted gritstone, it would make a memorable destination.

Tarnbrook Fell is where local red grouse are spattered by the copious gull droppings. They are also out-shouted by the raucous gulls, whose wailing or laughing calls will be heard for the next mile or two.

Elsewhere, the cock grouse makes itself heard, especially in March, when he is most vocal at break of day proclaiming his territorial rights with a song-flight, during which he crows loudly *ka ka ka kowak, kowak*. Feathers fly when two rival cock birds use their beaks and claws belligerently. Then in April, with birds paired and the female sitting eggs, a measure of peacefulness occurs.

The 'Pathfinder' maps will confirm what you see on the ground – that the track does not make an abrupt left turn at the skyline but crosses a syke (watercourse) on its way to Brown Syke. The route is waymarked by posts or small cairns. A post-and-wire fence is crossed by a particularly lofty stile.

Now, if there is clarity, you will gasp with delight at the panoramic view of the Three Peaks (Whernside, Ingleborough and Penyghent), sentinels of the limestone country, also Fountains Fell and, to the west, Gragareth, Casterton Fell and the Lakeland Hills. Further on, you may be able to identify the huge form of Black Combe, beyond Barrow-in-Furness.

Follow the side of the fence till it becomes a wall. Here there is another stile to be used. Follow the wallside till it becomes a wire fence and ultimately, with the sounds of gulls still in your ears, climb to Wards Stone, the attic of Bowland and somewhat reminiscent of the 'groughs' in the Kinder area of Derbyshire.

In clear weather, it is a stimulating experience to stand on Mr Ward's Stone, on which a post has been set, using a heap of large stones for support. The eye ranges around a

The summit of Wards Stone has an unrivalled view of the Bowland Fells.

horizon crowned by bare sheep ridges, empurpled with heather blossom in late summer.

There are two trig points, well separated. The easterly point, which you first encounter, is the true summit of the fell, being three feet (1m) higher than its partner, reached after trudging across a plateau where golden plover give their sad calls and run with mincing steps between tufts of coarse grasses. This grassy area is conspicuous in what is otherwise an expanse of heather.

Using the well-worn track from Wards Stone to Grit Fell on a hot, dry day in August, you will kick up white heather pollen at almost every footfall. The moorland is extremely well-managed. The peat is kind to your boots and muscular suspension. Nothing jars the spine. When crossing an estate access track, notice that there are tufts of heather (not the usual tufts of grass) at the centre of this remote, little-used road.

The route has areas of jumbled boulders, peat and heather reminiscent, as stated, of Derbyshire moorland. At Grit Fell, the miles

of purple bloom end with a fence and high stile. At the next good fence, notice the difference between heather moorland and one debased by sheep-grazing. Follow the fence side at the edge of Hare Appletree Fell to the Jubilee Tower (*walk 1*).

The final stretch of the journey is by a field path, via Westfield House, Lower Moor Head and Meeting House Farm to Abbeystead. From the Jubilee Tower, it is best to go to the first-named farm by the normal approach road, to avoid forcing a way through a mini-jungle of rushes. The concrete road through the farmyard continues to Lee Tenement, whence the footpath is easy to follow, taking a steady course to Abbeystead, with curlews and lapwings to entertain you.

At crucial points, the route is waymarked using yellow arrows. If you go in July, you will walk in fog (the sappy second growth, following mowing for silage or hay). To see a lime-yellow field in sunshine backed up by the blue-black of fells in shadow, with a big sky full of fascinating cloud formations, is invigorating to the spirit.

Of the old farms passed, Meeting House Farm is perhaps the most interesting, having been for many years a gathering place for Quakers. The meeting house itself was sold about thirty-five years ago for £1,000. The burial ground is infrequently disturbed. Use a stile in the wall to gain access to a short stretch of path known locally as the Duck Pad, striding along beside a small brook and crossing a wooden bridge into a big field.

Follow the yellow signs to Chapel House Farm, using the right hand of two waymarked gates. Bear left for a footbridge (not easy to see but about halfway along the tall hedge) and turn right for a gate leading on to the road, a little over half a mile (¾km) from Abbeystead.

WALK 4: ABBEYSTEAD AND THE UPPER WYRE

Start: Abbeystead. Grid Ref: 563 543
Distance: 3 miles (5km)
OS Maps: Pathfinder 659 (SD 45/55)
Walking Time: 1½ hours

Walk beside the Wyre on the outward course and return on a path which involves crossing wooden bridges over brooks in well-wooded cloughs, finally passing through some outstanding mature woodland. Neither the distance nor the terrain make this walk exacting.

Abbeystead, with its handsome buildings, several in Elizabethan style, exists largely to serve a huge estate of the Duke of Westminster.

The name 'Abbeystead' is derived from a monastery founded by monks from Furness, at the edge of what is now Barrow-in-Furness. These Cistercians found Wyredale somewhat damp and uninviting. By 1323, the area simply held a vaccary (where cattle were ranched).

In high Victorian times, the Earl of Sefton brought to Abbeystead the grandeur of a mansion built in the Elizabethan fashion. His lordship took up residence in 1886. (This mansion is not open to the public, though the gardens may be visited at prescribed times.)

Abbeystead is connected by bus with Lancaster but most walkers arrive by car, eager to explore a district of woods, cloughs and fells. The favourite starting point is by the isolated church beside the road west of the village.

Start in the village itself. Early summer is a good time for exploration, for then the extensive woodland has fresh foliage, rhododendrons are decked with blobs of colour and some especially deep purple foxgloves are in bloom.

Walk up the hill, heading west for a short distance. A wooden stile (left) gives access to a field, across which lies a sawmill. A concrete road is your route to the riverside.

The stretch of water which looks natural, having silted up, is Abbeystead Reservoir. A close view of the weir is possible by using a narrow wooden gate towards the end of the long wall (left) and walking a few paces along a well-beaten track.

You may also step on to the iron bridge for a view of the river and the rich foliage of alder, sycamore, rowan and birch. The alder, which is of considerable size, is a waterbank-loving tree which paddles when the river runs high.

Return to the concrete road and shortly you will see, near a concrete structure connected with the water authority, a memorial plaque relating to the tragedy in May 1984, when visitors from St Michaels-on-Wyre and employees of the water authority died when an explosion occurred in an underground chamber they were being shown.

This Wyre valley holds lush pastures, the summering ground of Friesian milk cattle and sucklers (beef cattle, some being a cross between the Friesian and Hereford breeds). Hillside woodland is well-represented by the indigenous types of tree. Thorn and elderberry are seen near the river. In early June, when the curlew have young, the anxious parents fly around with yelping cries.

In due course, the open ground ends with trees in evidence on three sides. Long Bridge, another metal structure, this one named after a local wood, is your crossing of the River Wyre. The near side of the bridge has a swing gate to deter footloose farm stock. Beyond the bridge is a foretaste of the beauty of the local

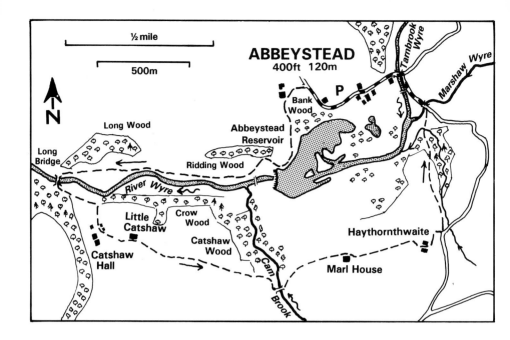

deciduous woods, with the steepled foxgloves evident among tall, lush grasses.

The path swings, crosses a brook by means of a wooden bridge, and settles down to an easterly course, climbing to offer good views of the valley, including the solitary church and the high fells. Beyond a gate, the path heads up the hill to the right and you will pass through the farmyards of Catshaw Hall and Little Catshaw.

In early summer, the Swaledale sheep are shorn by a team of men using mechanical shears. When the fleeces have been removed, the sheep are re-marked to indicate the farms with which they are associated. (Sheep also have a lug-mark; the term 'lug', meaning ear, originating as the law mark of the Norse folk of over 1,000 years ago.)

Beyond Little Catshaw, keep to a steady easterly course, eventually leaving the farm track for grassland to the left of a fence, giving access to Cam Clough, with yet another wooden bridge.

The joy of being in a fine tract of deciduous woodland is heightened by locating the ruins of a large building amid the greenery – what remains of a cotton mill destroyed by fire about the middle of the last century. A little further on is the dried up mill dam, thick with vegetation.

Yet another wooden bridge over a brook is negotiated; then there is a climb to Marl House (farm), with the view opening out to show the part of Abbeystead's splendid mansion.

The lower part of the valley seems to be almost continuous woodland, with well-timbered strips extending up the cloughs. From Marl House, follow an access road fringed by attractive and well-maintained thorn hedges.

Just beyond a group of stone buildings is a cattle grid. The route now descends to Hawthornthwaite. Walk to the hard-surfaced road and, within a few yards, you will see a small wooden gate with a footpath sign upon

The dipper, with its white bib and chocolate-brown plumage (which looks black from a distance), may be seen bobbing on stones where rivers run clear and cool.

it. This gives access to a path descending on open ground to the west of Bond Clough.

Eventually, the path enters Hinberry Wood, the path being narrow and winding, descending the steepest places by stone steps and crossing the wettest patches by inconspicuous wooden bridges.

The woodland resounds with the songs of warblers and the liquid calls of chaffinches. The path emerges on to the road associated with Doeholme Farm; turn left and walk across Stoops Bridge to Abbeystead village.

WALK 5: CHIPPING AND WOLF FELL

Start: Chipping. Grid Ref: 621 433
Distance: Excepting Wolf Fell, 3½ miles (5½km)
OS Map: Pathfinder 669 (SD 64/74)
Walking Time: 2 hours

This is a walk to undertake after visiting Beacon Hill Country Park and, among other things, picking up a leaflet dealing with access to the Bleasdale Fells, which are worthy of several visits. Wolf Fell is your 'optional extra' on an excursion which is best undertaken in late spring, when the woods and gills are misty with bluebells. Chipping has two handy (free) car parks. If the weather is variable, those who climb Wolf Fell (a feature on the access area) will need waterproof clothing and boots.

Chipping – the Chipinden (market) of *Domesday Book* – is popular with day-trippers. The village was just outside the old Forest of Bowland and it had a popular market. Chipping stands clear of tracts of mossland from which the black stumps of primeval oaks have been taken. The local river, which is called the Loud, joins the Hodder at Doeford Bridge.

The village has kept its old character while providing a good range of facilities. What is now a photogenic post office was the home of John Brabin, dyer and cloth merchant, who left money for the establishment of a school and almshouses.

The Sun Inn is said to be haunted by the ghost of Lizzy Dean, a servant lass. In 1835, she was engaged to be married to a local man, who married another, so Lizzy, aged twenty, hanged herself in the attic of the Sun. Her last request was that she might be buried under the path of the church, so that her former lover would have to walk over her when attending Sunday services.

Fell-walkers may ramble to their heart's content on the smooth and grassy Bleasdale Fells – Fair Snape (648 acres/262ha), Wolf Fell (514 acres/208ha) and Saddle Fell (360 acres/146ha). Those who wish to 'bag' the

highest summit should head for Fair Snape (1,674 ft/510m).

The fells are classified as an access area, which means that there are no public footpaths as such as access may be withdrawn at certain times, such as during the shooting season.

Few country churches have a more prominent position than St Bartholomew, Chipping, which is approached on an impressive flight of steps. A church stood on this site before 1230 but this is one of the churches 'improved' by the Victorians. You must look hard for traces of earlier times – the base of a cross, a piscina (basin) of the fourteenth century and chest of sixteenth-century date.

Leave Chipping on the road between a cafe and the church, bearing right at a Y-junction, which leads to what some local people refer to as the 'duckpond'. It is, in fact, the dam associated with premises where chairs are made. The chair factory, owned by H J Berry and Sons, has been in existence for over a century.

Chipping Brook rises below Wolf Fell. The dam has been colonised by mallard, and in spring the ducks swim with a flotilla of downy young birds paddling furiously behind them.

Beyond, the narrow road passes along a

46

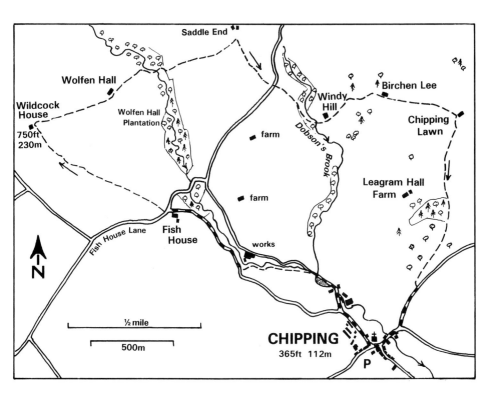

pleasant little valley which is semi-wooded
and has patches of gorse. On a still day in
spring, bird song is amplified as though in an
echo chamber. The roadside holds a profusion of butterbur.

Chipping is in the heart of the Lancashire
cheese country. Here the Procter family is
synonymous with cheese, one branch being
factors and another producing the crumbly
mild version of Lancashire cheese. When
Timothy Procter founded the Wolfen Mill
Dairy Company in 1934 it was to assist
farmers who were producing poor unpasteur-
ised cheese at home. White crumbly Lancashire is not a long-keeping cheese, but fatty
Lancashire has a longer life, maturing into
something stronger and sharper than the
best-known variety.

A path beside a modern housing development leads down to a bridge in a clough

which in spring is misty with bluebells. A
footpath across the road traverses some
squelchy woodland and it is preferable, for a
short distance, to use the road to Fish House,
stopping periodically to look down into the
clough and its massed bluebells.

Bear left (road marked Bleasdale) and
notice a footpath sign, right, which extends
across large pastures tenanted by curlews and
lapwings to the foot of Wolf Fell. Aim for a
ruined building (Wildcock House) and you
should find the gates and stiles.

At bluebell time, the lapwings are well on
with their nesting routine. Notice the back of
one of the crested birds when there is strong
sunlight. What appeared to be black is now
seen to be dark green (hence the name green
plover) which, should you get very close, is
seen to be shot over with purple. The
headcrest is longer on the male bird than the

47

female. If the eggs have hatched, the parents fly with wailing calls and occasionally dive with stiffened wings: the sound of air being displaced making a 'wickering' sound.

In the fields, tussocks of rushes in a line indicate the course of a brook. The rush occupies ill-drained or moist land. Looking towards Wolf Fell, you will undoubtedly see some hang-gliders circling around the summit like multi-coloured buzzards, but in their movements being cumbersome compared to the birds. The kestrel, which is not rare in Bowland, hovers with widespread tail and slow-moving wings as it scans the ground for incautious voles and mice.

On reaching the edge of Wolf Fell, you will see the well-worn paths ascending to the summit, where the hang-gliders are assembled. Climbing the fell is, as indicated, an 'optional extra'. You now traverse the edge of the fell, passing Wolfen Hall (notice the footpath sign on a gate in the farmyard).

The hall, a former manor house, was the home of John de Knoll of Chippindale. The de Knolls were eventually linked through marriage with the Shireburns, generations of whom were buried in the Shireburn Chantry (otherwise known as the Wolfhouse Quire) at Chipping Church.

The path from Wolfen Hall descends a rather steep slope into a clough and, as you climb the other side, offers a fine view of Wolf Fell. In spring, bluebells are profuse in an area now thinly wooded.

Ignore the stiles in the fence to the left, using the one lying directly ahead. The green mound and modernistic structure on the hilltop to the left is a reservoir. The beech plantation shields a view of Saddle End, where some walkers begin their ascent of the Bleasdale Fells.

A stile gives access to the approach road to the farm; across the public road is a wooden gate and a farm track which passes a fenced-in pond. Now you are contouring, by way of Windy Hill and Birchen Lee. The watercourses pass through bluebell woods. The well-farmed and contented countryside is sappy and green with rye grass, which in due course will be ensiled for winter feed for the cattle. On some pastureland to the left of

St Bartholomews Church, Chipping, is approached up a ponderous flight of stone steps.

48

Lapwings return to their high pasture nesting areas around the end of February. The tumbling display flight of a cock bird is a familiar feature of the Bowland spring.

what has become a concrete road is a profusion of mayflowers.

So to Chipping Lawn (which has a board named Laund Farm). The red and fallow deer of the past are but folk memories; the roe deer flits as inconspicuous as a shadow from wood to wood, not suited to being fenced in.

With concrete still underfoot, and park-like ground round about, commence the gradual descent, within easy viewing range of Leagram Hall Farm, to join the road north-east of Chipping village.

Leagram Hall (right), which is not open to view, occupies the site of a lodge at one of the old Bowland lawns (deer enclosures), what is now Leagram being dis-parked in 1556. In the sixteenth century, the old lodge, known as

the Lawn, was an illegal meeting place for Catholics, with hidey-holes provided for the priests in case representatives of the law arrived. Edward Arrowsmith, priest, paid the ultimate penalty – death by execution at Lancaster in 1628.

John Weld, who resided at Leagram Hall from 1850 until 1886, kept a diary in which he recorded details of natural history, such as the albino swallow – it was 'dull white without a single coloured feather about it' – observed in early autumn, 1856.

With park-like ground about you, the walk ends in a grand setting. The descent towards Chipping is a gradual one and takes you into hedge country. Beside the road, in spring, is the frilly white of cow parsley and the bright flowerheads of herb robert.

49

WALK 6: CROASDALE AND DUNSOP HEAD

Start: Slaidburn. Grid Ref: 712 524
Distance: 7¼ miles (11½km), climbing 1,000 feet (305m)
OS Map: Pathfinder 660 (SD 65/75)
Walking Time: 4½ hours

Wainwright, who compiled the pictorial guides for Lakeland and the Pennines, considered the upland route from Hornby and by Croasdale into Bowland as 'possibly the finest moorland walk in England'. You will have a brief encounter with it while passing between the heathered upper valley of Croasdale Brook and the cap of Dunsop Fell. Do not venture this way when there is low cloud or mist. Wear durable footwear and pack in your rucksack some waterproof clothing.

The walk begins beside Slaidburn green and close to a Wesleyan chapel (built 1821; restored 1889). At the prominent war memorial, bear right to cross over Croasdale Brook, the banks of which are colonised by butterbur. Beside the road is catmint (rub two fingers on a piece and then smell the minty aroma), meadowsweet and melancholy thistle.

The footpath sign (left) indicates a short, sharp climb towards a stand of sycamore, from which there are much-improved views of Slaidburn and the Hodder Valley. On the banks of Croasdale Brook are deciduous trees of great age – thorn, rowan and ash. The swallow, its long forked tail prominant in flight, and house martin, which is distinguishable by a white rump, nest at the buildings in this area, the swallows on beams and ledges in outbuildings, the martins under the eaves.

Near Shay House, the path joins the track leading to Croasdale House, a white-painted building. The present structure is a consequence of extending a seventeenth-century building on a sporting estate. The moors around Croasdale abound in red grouse.

Just beyond Croasdale House, a rough track is followed into the upper valley. The wooden bridge is not on the official right of way, which remains east of the water. Notice, on the near bank, a step stile in a post and wire fence.

But if Croasdale Brook is in spate, cross the bridge and follow the west bank for safety. Do not risk fording the brook – as you must, in due course – when there is a furious flow of water. The path is through an area of wet ground, with rush beds. The track is faint.

On a clear, sunny day in August, Croasdale glows with flowering heather and with the vermilion berries which adorn the many old rowans growing from high banks beside the brook.

Having forded the watercourse, keep to the left of a lightly-fenced plot (where a rain gauge once stood) and follow the slight track to a ruined outbuilding on the hillside to the left. Here, about 2½ miles (4km) from Slaidburn, is the House of Croasdale, now in a solitary, roofless state, with the wild moors about it. The building is far less imposing than its name implies, but its situation is impressive.

As your path contours the hillside, with coarse grasses or bracken beside it, scan a landscape which had its sharp edges removed by glacial action and was in turn scarred by quarrymen. The sporting nature of the estate is indicated by the simple butts (behind which shooters crouch awaiting a flypast of flushed grouse).

You shortly reach the old road connecting the valleys of Lune and Hodder. It is shown on the map as Roman Road but some know it as the Hornby Road. In part it ran along

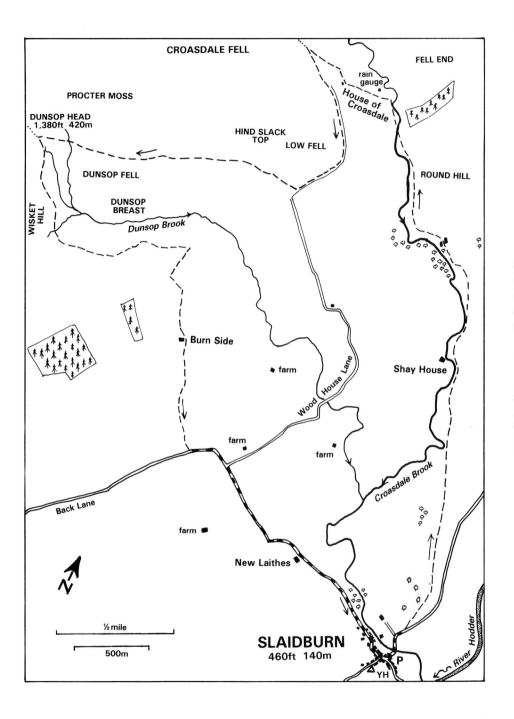

CROASDALE FELL

FELL END

PROCTER MOSS

rain gauge

House of Croasdale

DUNSOP HEAD
1,380ft 420m

HIND SLACK TOP

LOW FELL

DUNSOP FELL

ROUND HILL

DUNSOP BREAST

WISKET HILL

Dunsop Brook

Burn Side

farm

Wood House Lane

Shay House

farm

farm

Croasdale Brook

Back Lane

farm

New Laithes

N

½ mile

500m

SLAIDBURN
460ft 140m

P

YH

River Hodder

51

Upper Croasdale, a shallow valley between tracts of calluna moorland, which sustains both sheep and grouse.

the pre-1974 boundary between Yorkshire and Lancashire.

To others, what is undoubtedly an ancient way between High Salter and Roeburndale was used for the transportation of salt from the coast using packhorses. Salt was a vital commodity, especially when meat required for winter use was salted down to preserve it.

You first reach the Roman Road on a stretch where it is semi-tarmaced. The moorland extending to the right is well-tended for the benefit of grouse. In spring, hen grouse sit on their nests like feathered tea-cosies. A bird briefly leaves its nest, with its nine or so eggs, to drink. Otherwise she sits out the long days, keeping still and quiet and thus hoping to avoid detection by predators like the fox.

Leave the Roman Road, with its splendid long views over a gentler landscape, where an

old cart track goes off to the right. This is a steady 400 feet (120m) climb to Dunsop Head. The track has become deeply-sunk on the side of the fell. Water has scoured some of the ruts until they are many feet deep, so the route should be followed with care.

The track continues, deep-sunk between rushes, until a small heap of stones on a grassy moor marks the end of the climbing. On a sunny day you will find yourself in an area of bleached grasses under a big sky with impressive views of the upper Hodder and Slaidburn areas, also (on the northern skyline) the summits of Ingleborough and Penyghent.

The whistle of a golden plover may be heard, this species nesting on the fell. And everywhere are the Swaledale sheep, characterised by a black face and grey muzzle.

Slaidburn's grammar school dates from 1717, when it was endowed by a local farmer. Just over the wall from the school stands the church of St Andrew.

The wool of the Swardle (the local pronunciation) is tightly packed and does not become draggled in snow.

Before a drystone wall is reached, negotiate some bog or peat. Posts with yellow tips are the markers. The presence of the wall indicates what happens when sheep grazing is controlled. On the near side, the moor has degenerated to coarse grasses, with little heather and bilberry. Over the wall, the moor is dark, wine-red with heather blossom in season. The ideal is to have grouse and sheep in complimentary numbers and at a population level that does not take too much from the landscape.

Dunsop Head is the source of one of the minor rivers of Bowland. It begins with a gurgling of water among the 'rush-bobs'. Soon, as Dunsop Brook, it is flowing down a V-shaped cut on the fell.

A cart track leads off Dunsop Fell; it keeps to the high ground, crossing an area of white (grassy) moor before descending to a gate near Burn Side. The waymarked path goes to the east of the premises. In the wet ditch are catmint and watercress.

Turn left at the road, which is followed down to Slaidburn. This last stretch is in limestone country – look at the walls as a guide to the local geology. The plants on grassy banks include meadow cranesbill, meadowsweet, harebell, vetch, scabious, melancholy thistle and Welsh poppies.

WALK 7: BRENNAND AND THE TROUGH

Start: Dunsop Bridge. Grid Ref: 660 501
Distance: 8 miles (13km), climbing 1,200 feet (365m)
OS Map: Pathfinder 660 (SD 65/75)
Walking time: 4½ hours

Brennand lies at the heart of the Forest of Bowland and is approached through a dale which has affinities with a Scottish glen in its brawling river, heather, bracken and abundance of conifers. From Brennand Farm, the walker uses a sporting path, Ouster Rake, across to the Trough of Bowland. The return is beside a motor road which is not normally busy. Wear good footwear and take showerproof clothing.

On the green at Dunsop Bridge is a unique payphone – the 100,000th, and the most centrally situated in Britain. This modern kiosk stands on flags, flanked by rockery holding a variety of heathers. Wooden posts represent the four main points of the compass.

Cross the river bridge and turn right, passing a number of modern houses owned by the Forestry Commission and also the commission's office for Bowland. The River Dunsop is frequently in spate for it drains one of the wettest areas in England. Staple Oak and Whin Fell are the prominent hills to the left. The lower slopes are smothered in conifers, with heather on the higher slopes.

Beatrix Fell, on the opposite side of this deep little valley, has a conifer plantation. Roe deer flit like shadows where the woodland is thinner, and graze the field edges at dusk.

Dunsop Bridge, taking its name from an old crossing point of a boisterous river. The new-style telephone kiosk on the green is the most central if its kind in England – as an inscription relates.

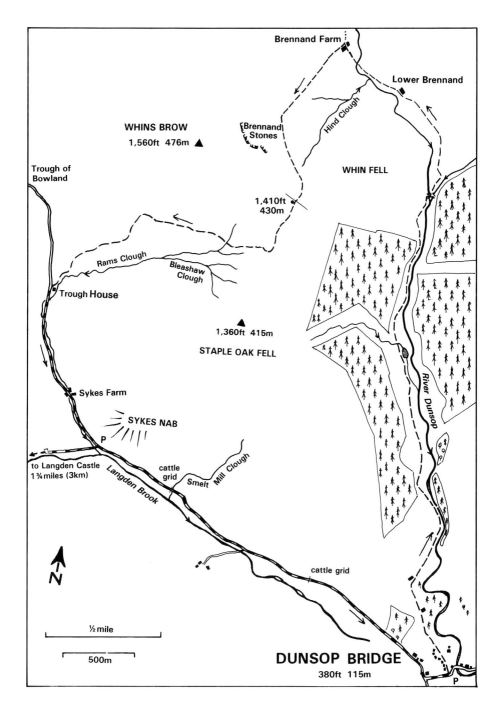

Brennand Farm

Lower Brennand

WHINS BROW
1,560ft 476m ▲

Brennand
Stones

Hind Clough

WHIN FELL

Trough of
Bowland

1,410ft
430m

Rams Clough

Bleashaw
Clough

Trough House

1,360ft 415m ▲

STAPLE OAK FELL

River Dunsop

Sykes Farm

SYKES NAB

P

to Langden Castle
1 ¾ miles (3km)

Langden Brook

cattle
grid

Smelt Mill Clough

cattle grid

N

½ mile

500m

DUNSOP BRIDGE
380ft 115m

P

The roe has a black moustachial stripe and a kidney-shaped rump patch. A buck (male) carries small, two-pronged antlers. If you hear a hoarse cough from the woods, it will almost certainly be the alarm call of a roe deer.

Sika deer, introduced to the Gisburn area early this century for sport, have spread widely and sometimes occur in the valley of the Dunsop. The sika is a medium-sized deer (as opposed to the roe, which is considered small) and it wears a summer coat of dappled chestnut which becomes browny-grey in winter. The antlers of the stag (male) are simple and branching, not unlike those of the red deer, a number of which were reported in the area in 1992. It was presumed they had escaped from captivity.

The unfenced road you are following crosses an area of lush sward and is then hemmed in by commercial plantations of mainly sitka spruce, a favourite of the forester because it grows quickly and yields good timber. The sitka was introduced to Britain in 1831 by David Douglas, the Scottish botanist, who found it growing on the coastal strip of British Columbia, Canada.

At the side of the River Dunsop are some venerable alders, a tree once prized for its wood, which was suitable for making the soles of clogs, then in demand by agricultural workers and also by those engaged in the textile industry. Large quantities of roughly-cut soles were sold to cloggers in the Lancashire towns.

The Scottishness of this valley is sustained by the profusion of gorse bushes alongside the river. It is said that when the gorse does not bloom, then kissing is out of favour. Its conspicuous yellow flowers are to be seen for most of the year.

Birds of the river include the dipper, a bird that looks black but is actually a very dark brown, with a white 'bib'. The dipper 'bobs' on a stone or walks underwater, its feathers looking silvery from air bubbles, while seeking food between and under the stones.

The presence of migratory fish – sea trout or salmon – is indicated by the presence of red-breasted merganser and cormorant, the latter, a large bird with black plumage and white face-patch, having commuted from the coast to share the feast. From a salmon hatchery in Bowland, young fish (smolts) are released and eventually find their way to deep water off Greenland, where they feed up, later returning to the home rivers, which they are said to detect by the distinctive blend of water. The average salmon spends about three years in the sea.

The road winds between banks of bracken, with conifers on the hillsides. A conspicuous house on the left is called the Bishops House, though little is known about it. In an area of silver birch (right) you may see the fly agaric, a (poisonous) fungus which is well-known because its cap, red with white spots, is a favourite with artists who illustrate fairy tales. Most self-respecting fairies and elves would not sit on the fly agaric.

The river flows through an area where it was dammed for the benefit of waterfowl, with mallard especially common. The valley floor is wet, and pools contain bogbean. The valley has its resident adders and grass snakes, both shy. The adder, our only poisonous species of snake, with a black zig-zag on its back, is not often seen. In a dry spell, it emerges from an afforested area to lie on boggy ground.

In 1967, when there was a 'cloudburst', the Dunsop River became a furious torrent and swept away a substantial borehole building which, ironically, had some marks cut on its side to indicate the heights reached by previous big floods.

Turn left into the Brennand Valley, which is lush green from meadowland, with two farmsteads and evidence of former mining. Green tracks extend across the hillsides to man-made caves – mine levels, driven far

Smelt Mill Cottages, once the destination of packhorse trains with loads of lead ore and now, in part, the headquarters of a voluntary rescue organisation.

underground to intercept the mineral veins. In the ore removed was lead and a good proportion of silver. (The mines lie off the official rights of way and, being dangerous now, should not be entered.)

The oldest mine sites are on the shoulder between the Brennand and Whitendale rivers. The name Good Greave relates to a mine. Mineral workings existed near Brennand House and Whitendale House.

It is related by Webster (1671) that gentlemen from London, who had been connected with mining about 1600, returned in 1655 to re-open those mines which had proved to be rich. The enterprise failed, 'they being men neither of free Purses to follow such a Work, nor of skill or government fit to manage such an Enterprise'.

The London men left, deserting their chemist, Walter Basby, who was an old man.

He was befriended locally and he told of his exciting past – how in the time of James I he had been sent to Russia to establish the standard of the Russian coinage and, while there, travelling to the mines in Tartary. Captured by the Tartars, he was ransomed by the Empress of Russia and continued his long career as an assayer of silver and lead.

Walk along the road to the dalehead farm. The path goes through the yard behind a building which stands where, in medieval days, there was a vaccary and cattle were ranched. Brennand once belonged to the monks of Whalley, who built and sustained a tiny chapel.

A path, marked by stiles, gates and way-marked posts, goes directly up the fell, passing near a rocky escarpment known as Brennand Stones. Looking back, you see the Brennand Valley in its completeness and also a shallow trough between Whitendale Fell and Middle Knoll. A public right of way extends through that trough to Whitendale Farm.

The route from Brennand to the Trough attains an elevation of over 1,100 feet (335m). Where it levels out, the path is peaty, and your boots will be whipped by heather. There begins a gentle descent through a less appealing type of landscape than the one you have traversed, but with the lofty Bowland ridges ahead for consolation.

The path is between extensive beds of rushes. Trough Barn (ruined) stands where there was a ford over a beck which has cut deeply into the ground and where there is a copse of mature trees, a good point to aim for during the descent of the fell. You will have a glimpse of the motor road passing through the conspicuous notch known as the Trough of Bowland.

The point of emergence on to the road is near Sykes Farm, which was yet another of the old Bowland vaccaries, then known as Glastirdale. In 1322, it was tenanted by Adam Langto. The name 'Sikes' has been in use since the fifteenth century, when the king drew rent from Thomas Boundes for 'Trogh and Sikes'.

The Parkinsons were among the residents at Sykes for generations (see the initials AP and the date 1692 on the datestone of a building now used as a barn). Eventually there was a community of nine small farms here, a number which had declined to five by 1845.

Where Langden Brook comes blustering down, a short walk from Sykes, you will see a fingerpost indicating a route to the Bleasdale Fells. On another day, if some gentle exercise is desired, walk along the straight, tree-girt road and continue on the track to Langden Castle, which is a grand name for a stone building once used as a sporting lodge.

The road to Dunsop Bridge is not normally busy. The time to avoid is a Bank Holiday. At Smelt Mill Cottages, the thirty-three year old Bowland Pennine Mountain Rescue Team has its headquarters. Its work embraces 240 square miles (620km^2) of fells from Winter Hill in the south to Caton Fell in the north. The largest area of open fell is that around the Trough.

Smelt Mill Cottages has an association with Brennand Farm, for the ore from Brennand and Whitendale was borne here by packhorses for smelting.

The Catholic church (right, beyond the cattle grid) is dedicated to St Hubert, patron of huntsmen. His image is fixed in stained glass. The church, opened in 1864, was paid for by Richard Eastwood, agent to the Towneley family.

WALK 8: DUNSOP BRIDGE, NEWTON AND THE HODDER

Start: Dunsop Bridge. Grid Ref: 660 501
Distance: About 7 miles (11km)
OS Maps: Pathfinder 660 (SD 65/75) and 669 (SD 64/74)
Walking Time: 4 hours

This walk takes in an area of hill farms and outbarns. It offers views of the Hodder Valley in an area known to the Victorians as Little Switzerland. The last stretch of the walk is close to the Hodder, switching banks at a simple (swaying) footbridge and returning to the south bank on an aqueduct. A little roadwork is necessary in the vicinity of Knowlmere Manor.

Park the car at Dunsop Bridge, a small village which has a picture postcard setting where the rivers Dunsop and Hodder blend their waters. Many of the farms have a royal connection through the Duchy of Lancaster. The latest type of telephone box has a floral setting on the green.

The walk begins on duchy property – a well-surfaced road, as straight as a bowshot. The River Dunsop flows to your left, its bank holding clumps of butterbur which in spring have lilac-pink flower heads and in summer ultra-large leaves, similar to those of rhubarb.

Just beyond a row of cottages, look carefully (right) for a path which zig-zags up a muddy slope between trees, roughly halfway between the cottages and the Weak Bridge. The path ends at a stile on a stretch of wall, beyond which is a large field.

This is curlew country. The response of the bird with the streaky-brown plumage and curving bill depends on the stage it has reached in its nesting programme. In spring, it skulks away from the nest before taking flight. In summer, when there are young, it will fly around, yelping.

Keep a little to the right of a line of electricity posts to reach Beatrix, a cluster of buildings named originally after a Norseman

of 1,000 years ago but now changed so it has a feminine association.

As you reach the approach road and pass through a gateway, notice a fine example of drystone walling on the left. Such a wall is really two walls in one, standing side by side, tapering with height (the batter) and held together with large stones called 'throughs'. The wall is surmounted by a row of 'top-stones'.

At Beatrix, the first of a number of yellow arrows waymark your route (you are moving clockwise; they were set up for someone going anti-clockwise). High Beatrix sees a parting of the ways. Ignore the left-hand yellow arrow and opt for that on a gate to the right, shortly coming in sight of one of the grand old outbarns of Bowland.

This structure is called (prosaically) Back of Hill Barn. In an older farming tradition, the outbarn held a stock of hay and had 'tying-up' for up to about a dozen young cattle, which remained here the winter through, gradually consuming the hay and being released from the barn daily to drink at the nearest spring. In due course, water troughs were installed.

A traditional hay meadow, in the days before artificial fertilisers were freely applied,

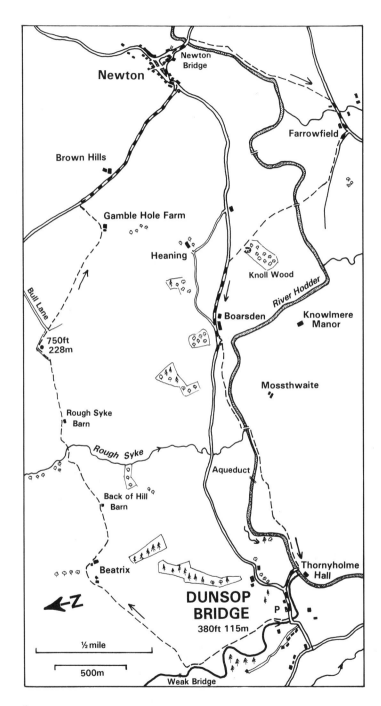

Newton Bridge

Newton

Farrowfield

Brown Hills

Gamble Hole Farm

Heaning

Knoll Wood

Bull Lane

River Hodder

Boarsden

Knowlmere Manor

750ft
228m

Mossthwaite

Rough Syke Barn

Rough Syke

Aqueduct

Back of Hill Barn

Beatrix

Thornyholme Hall

DUNSOP
BRIDGE

380ft 115m

P

½ mile

500m

Weak Bridge

was a wondrous sight. It might have had over fifteen species of grass – also sedges – quite apart from a variety of petalled plants. Modern rye-grass leys contain only rye-grass, plus a handful of individual weeds.

Few Bowland farmers make hay today. The grass is ensiled, converted into large bales and stored in black plastic bags, as you will see at the farms. Mostly, the bags of silage are stored outdoors (outbarns have become redundant) but at one farm on your route the barn is being used for storage of bags. It is vital that a bag should not be punctured and the air admitted or the silage will spoil.

A yellow arrow on a post beside the barn is so angled that it indicates the direction to be followed. Continue on grassland, descending to Oxenhurst Clough, where a fence is crossable at a stile. There is no yellow arrow here, but keep walking in the same direction, passing to the left of Rough Syke Barn and using a grassy track to reach the skyline, with a view northwards of Beatrix, Burn and Dunsop Fells – smooth and rounded, like recumbent elephants.

In summer, the oystercatcher, a pied bird which nests on the ground, stands out clearly from the Bowland meadows. Notice the long red bill, which resembles a stick of sealing wax, if you are old enough to remember what sealing wax looks like.

Enter a lane flanked by walls and gnarled thorn trees. Bear right. Where the track bears left, into Bull Lane, choose instead to pass through a small wooden gate and diagonally across a huge pasture to Gamble Hole Farm. Gamel, whose name the farm bears, was a Norseman. The 'hole' must have been one of many swallowholes, where soil and clay have been absorbed by fissures in the underlying

A limestone landscape between Dunsop Bridge and Newton, the last-named village having an old Quaker burial ground.

limestone, creating the effect on the surface of a grassy funnel.

A track connects the farm to the Newton road, which is flanked by hedges, mainly of thorn, with masses of bramble. In an area where limestone outcrops in many places, meadow cranesbill enlivens the roadsides in summer.This cranesbill, which loves dry grassland on limey soil, finds a well-drained roadside ideal and its blue-violet flowers are seen from June to September. Harebells, seen in summer, are the 'bluebells of Scotland' and, indeed, the flowers resemble bells, hanging on fine stems.

On the descent to Newton, notice the Quaker burial ground (right), and the Quaker meeting house (left), which was used from 1776 to 1988. The Quakers became established at Newton in 1670, and at what was once John Brabin's home, dated 1757, a school was established, one of the eighteenth century scholars being John Bright, who became a celebrated social reformer.

Newton (rendered 'Newtone' in *Domesday Book*) has seventeenth-century houses with dated doorheads, and a relatively modern village hall, in which 'old-time' dances are held, attracting enthusiasts from a wide area.

The Parkers Arms and Newton Hall stand on opposite sides of the road leading to the River Hodder. Cross the bridge and turn right, where a fingerpost is marked 'Farrowfield'. Above the river, in the nesting season, flit sand martins, which are light brown above, white beneath, with a dark brown stripe across the chest. They nest in burrows driven into sandy banks.

The path eventually parts company with the river, the last stretch being in a field near a barn at Farrowfield. The stile and a footpath sign is situated in a tall hedge. Cross the bridge over Foulscales Brook. All trace has been lost of the Foulscales Stone, with its early Christian emblems. The stone, which had been built into a wall, was taken to Knowlmere Manor for safe-keeping and subsequently misplaced.

Having crossed Foulscales Beck, count off two barns on the right, and then turn right (note a footpath sign) into a private road leading to Giddy Bridge. The stony road passes through a park-like countryside.

Knowlmere Manor, the principal house, was built in the Gothic style popular in late Victorian times. The name Knowlmere relates to Elias de Knoll, who owned the manor in the thirteenth century. A descendant married into the influential and wealthy de Hammerton family. When Sir Stephen Hammerton forfeited his estates, having taken part in the Pilgrimage of Grace, Knowlmere came into the possession of the Parkers. In due course, it was owned by the Duke of Buccleuch, whose family sold it to the Peel family.

Public footpaths give Knowlmere a wide berth, that to Giddy Bridge continuing over Hodder Bank Fell to Fielding Clough, with a return to Dunsop Bridge possible on the bank of the Hodder.

Our route continues by using a step stile just beyond a post-and-wire fence (right) and leads to a footbridge over the Hodder. The bridge is strung between piers made of brick and concrete. The staging is sound but the structure sways a little as you move.

Here is an opportunity to stay close to the Hodder. Beyond the bridge, the path goes through a lush green countryside, to the right of Knoll Wood, which covers a huge green mound, arriving at the side of the road between Newton and Dunsop Bridge.

Walk with care, in single file, and regain the riverbank at Boarsden Farm or a few hundred yards beyond, where there is a new step-stile. North of the Hodder becomes somewhat boggy. You might even flush a snipe, which has been probing in mud for food. Alarmed, the snipe will become airborne, uttering a vexed call – rather like a sneeze – and zig-zag aloft. A male snipe in its

The common snipe uses a fieldside post as a perch. This bird's aerial display in spring includes a dive, when air rushing through stiffened tail-feathers produces a goat-like bleating.

territory has a chipper, chipper call. In spring, a cock snipe, encircling its nesting area, occasionally dives in the chilly air, extends the stiffened outer barbs of its tail and produces a bleating sound.

It is a shock, during the riverside walk, to round a bend and see a huge white and grey painted bridge, rising like a mirage in the desert. The bridge (which you cross) was built by the water board in 1925 and carries water pipes over the river.

Beyond the bridge, complete the journey to Dunsop Bridge south of the Hodder, which flows serenely between well-wooded banks.

Thorneyholme Hall, once owned by the Towneley family of Burnley, was given to the Sisters of Notre Dame and became a nunnery. Thorneyholme is now a celebrated hotel. A bridge spans the river. The drive is flanked by wellingtonias, a species with a soft bark which was found growing in the Californian mountains about 1850. Three years later, the tree species had been introduced to England.

The Wellingtonia has enormous potential. One Californian specimen has a height of 272 feet (83m). It is possibly the tallest tree on earth.

WALK 9: AROUND STOCKS RESERVOIR

Start: Slaidburn. Grid Ref: 712 524
Distance: 11 miles (17½km)
OS Maps: Pathfinder 660 (SD 65/75)
Walking Time: 5½ hours

Stocks Reservoir, in the upper Hodder, is a prime area for birdwatching at any time of the year. Gisburn Forest, to the east, a creation of the Forestry Commission, includes among the fauna a small number of sika and roe deer. The walk is long but not over-demanding and, west of the reservoir, it follows the course of an old mineral line. At Slaidburn, use the car park near the Hodder Bridge.

Slaidburn village, of Anglian foundation, is drawn out and relatively thin, resembling a letter T with a long stem. The village stands near where Croasdale Brook joins the Hodder (a name meaning 'pleasant stream') and grew up beside a track leading to a ford.

In 1293, Henry de Lacy procured a royal charter for a fair to be held at Slaidburn on the first three days of August each year. Slaidburn, an important forest village, formed part of the West Riding of Yorkshire prior to the 1974 boundary revision. It is now in Lancashire.

On the green near the Hodder, a nineteenth-century maker of 'beaver' hats tacked out rabbit skins to dry. An upper room of the thirteenth century Hark to Bounty Inn (originally the Dog Inn) is still furnished with oak benches and a dock, a reminder of a forest court which dealt with minor offences and was used as recently as 1937. The present name of the hostelry was adopted in 1875 when the Rev Henry Wrigglesworth, a patron of the inn, while listening to the hounds giving voice in the street outside, exclaimed with delight, as he picked out the melodic sound of his own hound, 'Hark to Bounty'.

The church of St Andrew, of eleventh-century date, suffered badly from marauding Scots in the early fourteenth century. The Hammerton family contributed handsomely to the construction of the present church, which has a communion table instead of an

altar, in the spirit of the Reformation, and also a three-decker pulpit. A minor curiosity is a dog-whip, used in the days when some farmers took their dogs to church.

The adjacent building, Brennands Endowed School, dates from the early part of the sixteenth century and was once run by a master and usher. A charge was made for tuition in writing, accounts and Latin. The premises became an elementary school in 1876. Additions have been made at the rear, thus preserving the integrity of the facade. The children are transported to school from a large area of Bowland.

Leaving the car park, walk towards the centre of the village and bear right at a war memorial featuring a 1914-18 soldier with bowed head. A nearby garden (with seats) was made to commemorate the queen's silver jubilee.

Cross the bridge spanning Croasdale Beck and go (right) where an iron swing gate gives access to a brookside path. Bear left to cross the field, heading for a ladder stile to the right of a field gate.

Over the stile, walk along the edge of a large meadow and subsequently cross a single-span bridge, which is half-hidden by indigenous trees, including alder and thorn. A surfaced track leads to Hammerton Hall.

This river is the Hodder and, newly-released from Stocks Reservoir, its flow is regulated for the benefit of riparian owners.

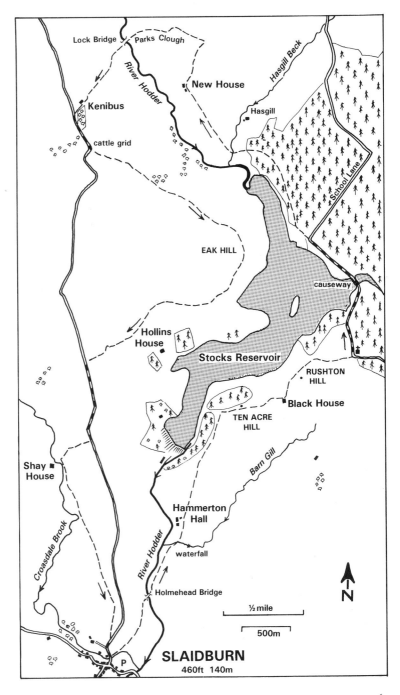

Lock Bridge   Parks Clough

River Hodder

Hasgill Beck

New House

Kenibus

Hasgill

cattle grid

School Lane

EAK HILL

causeway

Hollins
House

Stocks Reservoir

RUSHTON
HILL

Black House

TEN ACRE
HILL

Barn Gill

Shay
House

Hammerton
Hall

Croasdale Brook

River Hodder

waterfall

Holmehead Bridge

½ mile

500m

N

SLAIDBURN
460ft 140m

P

Local limestone was used in the construction of an old bridge, three-quarters of which has been washed away. What remains will fascinate those who have wondered how such a bridge was constructed.

Hammerton Hall, with its bays and mullions, was the property of a family associated with this area as early as the twelfth century and who were considerable landowners between Bowland and the city of York. A fine stone hall was built by Sir Stephen Hammerton, one of the (executed) rebel leaders in the Pilgrimage of Grace.

The present hall, commissioned by Oliver Breres, a Lancashire man who purchased Hammerton in 1548, is in the form of the Elizabethan E, made up of a gabled wing at either side and a central gabled porch at full height.

In the farmyard, where the barn's stone door-frames carry an attractive diamond pattern, is a fingerpost indicating (right) the direction to take. Then, at a Y-junction, bear left, a gatepost being waymarked with a small yellow arrow.

The field path climbs steadily to a wooden gate on the skyline. The view opens out to reveal some of Bowland's long, heathery ridges, including Beatrix Fell, Dunsop Fell and Croasdale Fell.

Beyond the gate, the landscape is largely afforested, with plantations and clear-felled, re-planted areas where the old flora has asserted itself. In summer there are bright patches from the flowers of the rosebay willow herb, a plant which the Victorians grew for decorative purposes. This species is certainly decorative, having purple flowers. Even the seed heads are appealing, being fluffy white. Rosebay willow herb was to be found growing wild in England from about the year 1860, its spread being hastened by its partiality for colonising dry areas of waste ground, such as near railways. Passing trains waft along the seeds and speed up dispersal.

The footpath from Hammerton Hall to the edge of Stocks passes a small oak wood. At Black House, which wa. sufficiently high above the proposed water level to remain when others were submerged by the new reservoir, you reach a farm track leading to the road.

Now join the road and, with Dalehead Church on the right, walk on to where the road has tall walls on either side. Peep over the left-hand wall for a view of Stocks Reservoir and then over the right-hand wall to see where Bottoms Beck flows into a lagoon fringed by sallows (willows). A picnic area, with information boards, has been established by the road (left).

Stocks Reservoir, which is visible from this point, was built between 1923-32 to provide water for the thirsty Fylde. The reservoir was named after the 'lost' village of Stocks-in-Bowland, which was demolished, the church (opened as recently as 1852) being pulled down and the stones used to build another church at a higher site (1838).

In times of drought, an island in Stocks becomes a promontory and the stone cladding on the reservoir's earth dam is visible. The island, a major black-headed gullery, has also been used for nesting by Canada geese, the population of which has risen to over 400 birds. You will almost certainly see and hear some of these attractive waterfowl.

Canada geese, introduced into Britain for sport, proved to be too tame but splendidly adorned the grounds of stately homes – until they became too numerous. The Stocks colony has thrived in recent years. Most of the geese nest on the nearby moors and the parents lead the goslings down to the reservoir.

Gisburn Forest, planted by the Forestry Commission on the eastern catchment area of Stocks Reservoir, has the monotony of sika spruce plantations relieved by the bright green of blocks of larch, a nesting place of sparrowhawks. This fierce predator of small

Burdock, which has large, hairy seed-cases. They stick to any creature which brushes against the plant.

Stocks Reservoir, in the making of which an old hamlet and several farms had to be demolished.

birds surprises and flies down upon its victims. The male sparrowhawk, which is grey with reddish-barred underside, takes food to a plucking post, from where it is collected by the female, a larger bird than her mate and having a dark brown mantle, the lighter breast being barred with brown.

Stocks Reservoir is on a trans-Pennine flight line for wild birds. The variety of habitats attracts many nesting species and it is a prime area for duck. Mallard and teal are seen throughout the year. In winter, the duck include tufted, pochard, goldeneye and wigeon. The wigeon population may be high and birds waddle ashore to graze with their short, stout bills. Disturb some wigeon and you will hear a distinctive two-tone whistle, *wree-ou*.

Cormorants arrive from the coast to fish for trout. Whooper and Bewicks swans, refugees in winter from the rigours of the northlands,

occur at Stocks but prefer the floodwaters of Ribblesdale near Long Preston.

Where the Hodder joins the reservoir is a moist, rushy area, ideal for ground-nesting birds. The edge of the reservoir attracts sandpipers and occasionally a pair of ringed plover is found nesting here. The coot, a squat water-bird which is dark with a white frontal disc (hence the saying 'as bald as a coot') builds a twiggy, waterside nest in areas with cover. Shingle banks are used by nesting oystercatchers, the eggs toning remarkably well with the shallow saucer-like depression in which they are laid, with minimal nesting material.

Breeding in the district are the red-breasted merganser and goosander, which are 'sawbills', having serrations to their beaks which enable them to keep a tight grip on any fish they catch. These ducks nest in cavities, such as holes in trees, not far from water. It was as recently as the early 1970s that goosanders began to nest in Lancashire.

The shore vegetation of Stocks is of a type adapted to fluctuating water conditions, and includes water purslane and common mudwort. Where the Hodder enters the northern end of Stocks Reservoir, a rush named *Juncus f)lliformis* grows extensively.

Go through a swing gate beyond the picnic area and continue along a well-beaten track with a wall on the left. The waymark post has two bands, – white and red – and is related to one of the information boards at the picnic area.

Foxgloves which seeded beside the massed trees are drawn up by the light and attain heights of over seven feet (2m). In marshy parts of Gisburn Forest grows the common sundew, an insectivorous plant with strikingly red leaves. In the forest is New Zealand willow herb, like a small pimpernel, with rosebay flowers. This may have been introduced with imported roadstone, spread to give the tracks a durable surface. A plant of improved ground is the great bellflower, which grows up to five feet (1½m) in height and may have twenty or thirty bells. The greater fleabane has a mass of grey hairy leaves.

The forest goes through rapid cycles of planting, growth, windblow or clear-felling, and re-planting. Unfortunately, most of the old farms and barns where I used to watch barn owls have been demolished. Here the barn owl, essentially a bird of open ground, once managed to combine that habitat with sorties along the rides of the conifer forest where there was usually an abundance of field voles. When an owl perched on the window-ledge of a barn, I took in details of its appearance – the light plumage, heart-shaped face and legs. The owl gives the impression that it suffers from knock-knees.

The path is flanked on the right by a row of western hemlock. The waymarking and colour-coded post indicate a turn to the right but, instead, go straight ahead, passing to the right of a barn-like building and some ruins. Follow a grassy path in an avenue formed by conifers and, at a wooden swing gate, gain the open ground.

The path bears right over a stone bridge, and begins a steady climb to New House in a landscape holding tufts of rushes and a few thorn trees. At New House, one building is ruined and the other held up partly by metal 'ties'. Continue to New Laithe and Catlow, on a track from which there are wide views. In summer, suckler cattle graze in the manner of the Norsemen's stock of 1,000 years ago.

This route does not actually reach Catlow. The map shows the path descending along the northern side of a wooded gill and across the Hodder to join a well-metalled way leading to the Slaidburn-Bentham road, near Kenibus, which stands in an area of ancient alders.

Turn left at the motor road. After a short distance – and just before a cattle grid is reached – turn left again, using a gate which gives access to a track passing to the right of a barn. Now look for a gateway, beside which is the remnant of a wall and also a metal fence. Almost immediately beyond this gate, bear right for the start of the trackbed of an old mineral line, installed to obtain stone from Jumbles Quarry on the fell beyond the Cross of Greet (raised at the division of two counties).

You will not stray from the trackbed for the next few miles, except where there are runnels, formerly bridged by wooden structures which have perished or been removed.

Leave the trackway at a fingerpost directing you to the right, up a grassy slope. The path joins the Slaidburn-Bentham road, which should be left with a right turn towards Shay House. Just short of the farm and before crossing a bridge over Croasdale Brook, use a stile (left) giving access to a field path which leads directly back to Slaidburn.

WALK 10: TO WHELPSTONE CRAG

Start: Tosside. Grid Ref: 769 561
Distance: 6½ miles (10½km), climbing 750 feet (230m)
OS Map: Pathfinder 660 (SD 65/75)
Walking Time: 3½ hours

This walk demands a fair amount of effort on rushy ground, with the occasionally boggy area. It is worth the effort because of its wilderness flavour, with massed conifers and grassy, sheep-decked moors. Don good footwear and do not expect to keep it dry. Try to avoid going on a humid summer day, when you will have a cloud of flies about your head. The return from Whelpstone is in part on a firm but unmetalled Forestry Commission road.

The easiest of the forest walks begin at the picnic area beside Stocks Reservoir (*walk 9*). The Whelpstone Crag expedition, which begins at Tosside, is more of a safari. The path is not always good to see. One section – between Tenters and Geldard Laithe – is not as shown on the OS maps!

However, persevere and you will have an afternoon to remember, with good views of Ingleborough and its neighbouring peaks (to the north) and Pendle Hill (in the south). Also in view is Stocks Reservoir and the upper Hodder Valley.

Tosside, the name of which has been associated with the fox, was a village dissected by the 1974 boundary revision. The church is in Lancashire and what was the vicarage – just across the road – stands in the North Riding of Yorkshire. There are separate local government services and mobile libraries, also separate community charges. In 1992, the Tossiders living on the Yorkshire side of the village were paying £100 less than the Lancastrians.

Tosside has its church, formerly Hoghton Chapel, where the simple Jacobean pews are marked by the initials of old families. Mount Sion Chapel, of the Old Independency, has changed hardly at all since its construction in 1812. Within one building are the chapel and the manse. I have taken services there in

winter, when a coke stove burned cherry-red. At a wedding – a rare event – the bride was warned not to go too close to the stove or her veil would be sucked towards it and shrivelled by the heat.

The walk begins near the inn, once the Temperance Hotel and now the Dog and Partridge. When dances are held in the community hall, some of the supporters start the evening at the inn and then simply cross the road. In former times, the stove which was used to heat the hall for a dance was removed just before the band struck up, two men slipping long metal rods through either side of the stove and taking it to a spare part of the car park.

Bailey Lane is the starting point for this walk. In dry weather, it will deposit white lime dust on your boots. The sides of the road hold an abundance of thistles, which attract butterflies, notably the small tortoise-shell, which has speckled orange and black wings. This species is particularly fond of nettles, on which it lays its eggs.

One of the industries that has sprung up to deal with felled timber is a sawmill (left). The massed sitka spruce are, when mature, some-what lacking in wildlife or botanical interest. Sitka spruce is popular with foresters because it is tolerant of wet conditions, and, though prone to windblow when it is twenty or more

Tosside, a hilltop village with a name said to be derived from the fox. Such a creature is represented on the weather vane shown in the picture.

years old, is less so than the Norway spruce. In good conditions, a sitka spruce may exceed 100 feet (30m) in three decades.

The Norway spruce, popular as a Christmas tree, was introduced into England from Scandinavia as long ago as the sixteenth century. The needles have four sides and end in a point, while the cylindrical cones have tightly-compressed papery scales. Its advantage over sitka spruce is that it continues to thrive in frosty conditions.

Of the local deer it is the sika that arouses most interest. This is an introduced species, originally in the Gisburn area. It spread to the newly-conifered ground near Stocks Reservoir. In what looks like unpromising country, the deer lie up in frost-pockets, where tree growth has been stopped or checked. They feed mainly at dawn and dusk, a popular area being in the area of Bottoms Beck.

The sika is a medium-sized deer, with simple branching antlers and a coat which in

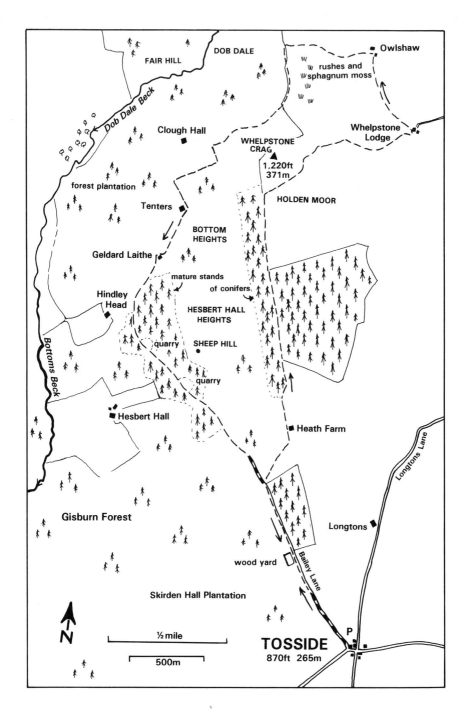

FAIR HILL

DOB DALE

● Owlshaw

⋎⋎ rushes and
⋎⋎sphagnum moss

Dob Dale Beck

Clough Hall

Whelpstone
Lodge

WHELPSTONE
CRAG
1,220ft
371m

HOLDEN MOOR

forest plantation

Tenters

BOTTOM
HEIGHTS

Geldard Laithe

mature stands
of conifers

Hindley
Head

HESBERT HALL
HEIGHTS

quarry

SHEEP HILL

Bottoms Beck

quarry

Hesbert Hall

● Heath Farm

Longtons Lane

Gisburn Forest

Longtons ■

wood yard

Bailey Lane

Skirden Hall Plantation

N

½ mile

500m

TOSSIDE
870ft 265m

P

summer is of chestnut hue, dappled with white, and in winter is a less attractive browny-grey. The deer has a prominent caudal (rump) disc that is heart-shaped; the long hairs of this disc can be erected when the animal is excited or alarmed, until it is as large and bushy as a powder puff.

Before the forest developed lustily, I could 'glass' deer from Bailey Lane. Also in view at that time were short-eared owls and, at dawn and to a lesser extent in the late afternoon, in spring, one might hear the hissing and cooing of black grouse at the lek (assembly ground) where it was every cock bird's ambition to reach the dominant area of the lek as the females (known as greyhens) arrived to be mated. The planting of trees broke up a large lek into several smaller ones, at which there would be only half a dozen birds. Now the black grouse is uncommon.

Where Bailey Lane has two subsidiary tracks, choose the right hand one, which is gated. Notice a stile in the fence to the left of the gate. Join the track to Heath Farm, seeing (on the horizon to the east) the distinctive outline of Ryeloaf, one of the hills dominating the small, secluded valley of Stockdale near Settle.

In summer, there are bird commuters from urban areas – swifts, which are small, dark and streamlined. The swifts are hawking insects above the forest and, when feeding their young, the insects are fixed by saliva into a nourishing ball of food. Swifts, which spend the greater part of their lives on the wing, give high-pitched squeals as they skim through the warm air.

Beyond Heath Farm, a stile in a wall marks the start of a thickly conifered area. Stay just outside the (frequently-gapped) drystone wall and you will find there are wooden step stiles at strategic places. The path is not over-used, but your eyes will quickly be attuned to the trail of those who have gone before you.

For a time there is forest on either side; then the path reaches the edge of Holden Moor, which now is damp and covered with coarse grasses and rushes but, within living memory, had a good covering of heather and therefore was valued as a preserve for red grouse, which were driven over the butts in the autumn.

The footpath, such as it is, stays on the near side of the hill. There is no public right of way on Whelpstone Crag, which now looms before you, surmounted by gritstone boulders, a triangulation pillar of the Ordnance Survey, and sheep and lambs which, in summer, 'lig up' in the shade of the rocks. The name 'Whelp Stone' is intriguing and may, like Tosside, have something to do with foxes – or perhaps even wolves.

Whelpstone Lodge and Owlshaw Lodge are served by a cul-de-sac road several miles in length which begins at Rathmell. In tracing the path back to the Forest from Owshaw Lodge Hall, let the walls be your guide. The landscape is otherwise featureless. Stay away from dense beds of rushes, which conceal boggy gutters.

On reaching the forest fence, follow it along until, near Whelpstone Crag, where a wall extends into the forest, you locate a step stile, and beyond it a strip of land relatively clear of growth. You have to bend your back here and there to pass under a few trees toppled by the wind.

The official path is shown on the map, but it is not easy to trace it amid the tangle of felled areas or close-packed trees. I prefer to stick to the forest road. Turn left where the road joins another metalled road and, in summer, is fringed by ragwort. Look at the EWS (emergency water supply) in case there are any dragonflies in the air.

The quarry areas you will pass (left) are good places to look for varied plantlife and small mammals (the rabbit is here, of course). Birds of the forest include the goldcrest, the smallest bird in Britain, being a mere two and a half inches (6¼cm) long. The goldcrest has a dull green plumage but sports a bright

Whelpstone Crag, the highest point on a ridge which is now, in part, a commercial forest. Both sika and roe deer are seen in this area.

headcrest which is bordered by black stripes. The crest is orange in the middle on the male, and lemon-yellow on the female. Agile and restless, the goldcrest is not easy to see as it feeds in the tree tops, but its thin, high-pitched, rapid song is distinctive. Someone described it as like the sound made by a fairy's spinning wheel. The goldcrest slings its hammock-like nest under the branch of a conifer in a well-sheltered spot.

The chaffinch, our commonest finch, its appearance being well-known from its tameness in urban areas, has a length of six inches (15cm). The chaffinch's cheery call, frequently heard in the forest, sounds like *pink, pink*. Hedge sparrow and titmice help to infuse a little life into the area.

Bailey Lane takes you back to Tosside, offering *en route* a view of the upper Hodder and Stocks Reservoir.

WALK 11: WHITEWELL AND BROWSHOLME

Start: Whitewell. Grid Ref: 659 469
Distance: 7 miles (11km), climbing 1,100 feet (335m)
OS Maps: Pathfinder 669 (SD 64/74)
Walking time: 4 hours

This is a walk on velvety grassland and pastureland, the haunt of nesting curlew, lapwing and even ostercatcher. You will have extensive views of the Bowland Fells. The walk enters two notable estates – the Duchy of Lancaster and Browsholme Hall. It is an exacting walk, with little shelter possible en route. In meadows, keep – where possible – to the wallsides, shut the gates after you and keep any dogs on a lead. Parking is usually possible in Whitewell near the parish church of St. Michael.

The area to be explored, once known as Little Bowland, includes the hamlet of Whitewell, on a bank of the River Hodder which sweeps around the foot of New Laund Hill, the setting for some 'fairy holes'. The Hodder gorge, deep and well-wooded, has fossiliferous limestone and also scarps of millstone grit.

Whitewell is a delectable spot, set beside a gorge in which the pearl-grey of limestone shows between a mass of trees. Walls hold crinoids, the fossilised remains of animals which populated a shallow sea over 300 million years ago. The district has grassy paths and woodland in which the pied flycatcher and long-eared owl are just two of an assembly of interesting birds.

Whitewell's large hotel is on the site of the manor house of Walter de Urswyck, keeper of Bowland Forest. It was the setting for Swainmote and Woodmote forest courts, where fines were imposed for such crimes as the unlawful felling of timber and hunting of deer. A saddler named William Isherwood was fined 'for felling a great alder, three small alders and four hollins [holly trees]'.

The fifteenth-century wayside chapel-of-ease, predecessor of the present large church, was built at the instructions of Keeper de Urswyck. Standing beside a wild stretch of the Clitheroe-Lancaster road, the chapel was doubtless visited by wayfarers about to pass

through the Trough of Bowland and anxious to placate the Almighty and ensure a safe journey. Whitewell was once served by a curate from Whalley, and Whitewell folk attended the parish church at Clitheroe for marriages and funerals.

Like many rural churches, St Michaels may be locked except on Sundays and special occasions. (The vicar, who now has several parished, lives at Chipping.) Nearby is the Inn at Whitewell, the substantial range of buildings overlooking the Hodder.

Cross the road from the church and continue up the hill, with the white-painted building on the right. The footpath sign is clearly visible, not far away, on the right of the road. Once you get up the steps and through the gate, in an area where three paths are marked on the map, finding the route to Radholme Laund can be confusing. The isolated building (Seedhill Cottage, close to a fenced-off waterworks tunnel) is your marker; pass it and then go straight up the hill, to where a wooden board (marking the location of a stile) protrudes above wall level on the skyline.

Look back towards the valley for a sweeping view that includes lightly-wooded New Laund Hill, beyond which lies Fair Oak, one of the high fells of Bowland. The Hodder meanders through a fertile valley. Each bend of the river is marked by a shingle bank. The

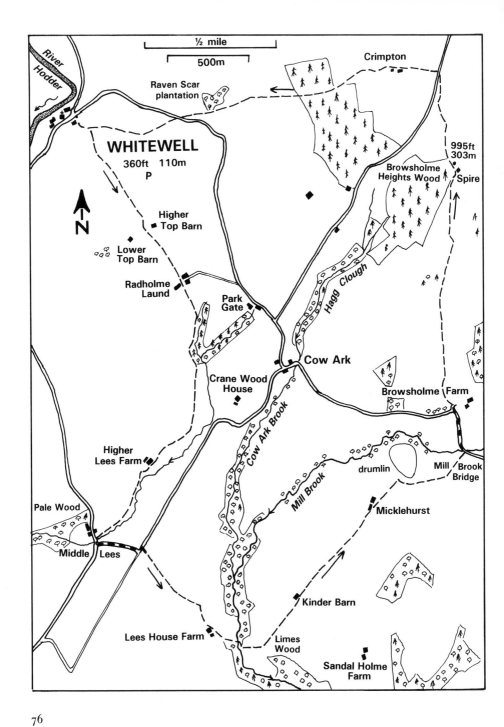

bridge between Whitewell and Dunsop Bridge is so high-arched that it appears to be standing on tiptoe.

Beyond the stile, the way lies unrelentingly uphill; bear right to a drystone wall and follow it to an iron gate, which gives access to a field. Keep to the wallside until you are close to a large outbarn. The wall you have been near is seen to have a substantial wrought-iron gate and attendant swing gate for pedestrians. When through here, walk diagonally to a stretch of wall between the two barns, heading for a wrought-iron gate and swing gate.

Go down the field, keeping the wall on the left, until you have reached Radholme Laund, named after a deer enclosure established on sweet limestone country in the thirteenth century. Now there is a large, well-managed farm.

Incidentally, the medieval deer park was bounded by a ditch eight feet (2½m) wide and four feet (1.25m) deep, the displaced material forming a bank on the outer side. Into the bank was driven a fence consisting of pales (split oak), augmented by a hedge of thorns.

The park-keeper's simple wood-and-thatch lodge became a stone building in the sixteenth century and has now developed into a large house. In modern times it was visited by the queen (who has a special interest in this part of Bowland through the Duchy of Lancaster).

Pass through the farmyard, using the metal gates. Note the elegant front of the farmhouse (which has a fairly steep roof, with pantiles of a light shade) and the large garden, in which there are no less than seven yew trees. Another metal gate leads into a field and set in the wall to the right is a further gate. You are now walking beside Crane Wood; in places it is misty with bluebells, and the pheasant is a conspicuous member of the local fauna.

Follow the wallside beside the wood and encounter a stile (beside which, there are the

Wild garlic, with its showy white blossoms and strong oniony smell, grows in shady, moist areas by road and river.

remains of an ancient thorn tree, sprouting a single living branch). Look behind you for a good view of high fells which, from a distance, resemble a brown ridge tent and include Wolf Fell, Burnslack Fell and Fair Oak Fell. Ahead of you now is an untrammelled view of Longridge Fell, with its stubble of conifers.

The stile is the first of a number of stiles leading through the fields and by the brook. The brook runs through a deep little valley and is fringed here and there by the ubiquitous butterbur. The straight stretch of road to the east of this path is the Roman road between Ribchester and Overborough. Most of the road is now under tarmac.

Having crossed a stile to the left of a field gate on the way to Higher Lees Farm, you will find that the farmer has posted up some simple signs marking the line of the path, basically along a primrose-adorned bank of the brook to where a new bridge has been built at Middle Lees. Stiles indicate the way. Beside the new bridge is a mini-jungle of wild garlic and butterbur.

77

Stepping stones have been placed in the brook. When you have gone up the bank to the road, a footpath sign will be seen. Branch off left, on a road flanked in spring by dogs mercury and celandine. The fields have been greatly improved for farming by ploughing, re-seeding and fertilising, but mayflowers are still to be found in the lush greenness. On joining the straight Roman road, turn left, then almost immediately right. In view is a sign indicating Lees House Farm.

The approach track is excellently maintained, crossing a green and contented countryside where curlew and lapwing nest. The farmhouse has a datestone (1678) above a doorway, though the present building looks somewhat younger than the stone.

A sporty part of the course begins at Lees House. As you pass through the farmyard you will see (a few yards across from a big blue slurry tank) a metal gate, giving access to a grassland near a cottage. A gap in the wire fence to the left is the start of the path which descends (slitheringly) through woodland (more bluebells, more garlic) to a wooden bridge over a brook.

Stiles permit you to enter a field. Your route is beside a shallow ditch (holding patches of marsh marigolds) to a large barn; the track connects the barn with the farmhouse of Micklehurst and on to the road near Browsholme Hall.

A sign across the road indicates whether or not Browsholme Hall is 'open to view'. Those who visit the old home of the Parkers, who have been associated with it since 1507, see

Browsholme Hall, a substantial house, reflects the importance of the Parker family in the area. Built in 1507, it was re-faced with red sandstone in 1604. The hall is open to the public at prescribed times.

a building which has the glow of mellowed pink sandstone. Here is an Elizabethan facade, a Queen Anne wing and a west wing recast by Sir Jeffrey Wyatville in 1805. The main doorway is part of a projection rising to the top of the building and incorporates pillars in three orders of Greek architecture – Doric, Ionic and Corinthian. (The effect is not unlike that of Stonyhurst College.)

Ignore this approach to Browsholme Hall and walk along the side of the road, passing between two houses, to attain another entrance to Browsholme, with signs. Just off the road, a metal gate is seen (left) and the path runs alongside a line of trees.

You are now heading northwards to Spire, the 'spire' being a lofty and thick wall erected by the Parker family as a landmark. It is attached to a farmhouse which was formerly on the Browsholme estate. Spire is in view for much of the way. The course of the footpath is at the rear of the farmhouse. Stiles give access to a large pasture, and the path eventually reaches the road after passing through a small area which has been planted with trees, the precise route indicated by stiles.

Across the road is the track leading to Crimpton Farm. Go between the buildings, and pass through a gate and over a stile to gain the open ground. The path goes towards the left of the group of beech trees, and extends beside a wire fence between pasture and conifer plantation to where a stile gives access to a very sloppy stretch of path cutting through the north side of the wood.

Now it is a downhill walk, with curlews and lapwings for company. Keep to the left of a small copse and find a stile just to the left of the second cluster of trees. Eventually the road is crossed. Notice the outcropping limestone and (near the field gate, just beyond the road) the remains of a large limekiln.

The path descends on familiar ground to Whitewell.

WALK 12: SAWLEY AND THE RIBBLE GORGE

Start: Sawley. Grid Ref: 774 466
Distance: 10 miles (16km)
OS Maps: Pathfinder 669 (SD 64/74) and 670 (SD 84/94)
Walking time: 5 hours

Between Sawley and Gisburn, the Ribble Way passes through a gorge which provides scenery on a grand scale, with well-wooded cliffs. Deciduous woodland offers shelter from the summer sun. The river life is varied. Roadside parking is possible at Sawley, to which we return through fields on the west of the river.

Sawley has been spelt variously down the years, examples being Salley, Salleyam, Sally, Sawlley and Sallay. Whichever name you use is derived from 'field of sallows' (willows).

It was in 1147 that Abbot Benedict and twelve Cistercian monks arrived to establish an abbey. Little remains of their enterprise but the well-tended ruins are worthy of a visit. (No charge is made for admission.) Notice the medieval archway which is now framing an ordinary field gate; it used to span part of the nearby road.

Park the car at the roadside where it is wide and walk towards Sawley Lodge. The first stretch of the walk is along the tarmaced approach road to the Lodge, with the Ribble a field's length away. At the approach to a stone gateway, you will see a notice prohibiting further progress along the tarmac way.

The Ribble Way, which we follow to Gisburn, bears left into a field, then left over a single wooden bridge spanning a ditch and into a large field. Bear right for the Ribble Gorge.

In spring, the big fields are enlivened by the calls of waders, including curlews and lapwings. Sika deer frequent the woods and are sometimes seen grazing at the field edges at dusk.

The ditch has a profusion of plant life, including water mint, meadow sweet and the greater birdsfoot trefoil. Cross some marshy ground by a plank bridge, walking with care along the side of a grassy slope, and even-

tually – having crossed some wooden stiles – reach the riverside, where the trailing stems of water crowfoot are visible.

In spring and early summer, the river is bird-busy, with sand martin, dipper, grey wagtail and mallard. The red-breasted merganser is a big, powerful duck with a shaggy green head which looks as though it would benefit from being combed. The bird is one of the 'sawbills', its mandibles having serrated edges whereby it can hold on to fish. It is only during the past thirty years that the merganser has colonised the Bowland watercourses. It nests among tree roots not far from the river.

A thickly-wooded tract across the river is part of the grounds of Bolton Hall, a former home of the Pudsays which was demolished in recent times. The vegetation seen from the riverside includes snowberry, originally planted to provide good cover for pheasants.

Pudsay's Leap, the first big cliff to be seen during the riverside walk, lies across the Ribble. William Pudsay (1556-1629), squire of Bolton-by-Bowland, owned the silver mine near Rimington but did not divulge to the State the silver he removed from it. In due course, representatives of the law arrived at Bolton Hall to apprehend him. Pudsay escaped on a horse, leapt over the cliff (an unbelievable feat) and rode off to the king, who – according to the old story – pardoned him. (*See walk 15 for the story of 'Pudsay's Shilling'.*)

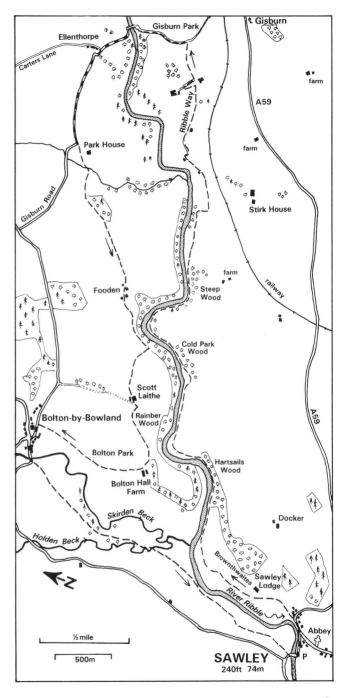

Gisburn Park

Ellenthorpe

Carters Lane

Gisburn

A59

farm

farm

Park House

Gisburn Road

Ribble Way

Stirk House

farm

railway

Fooden

Steep Wood

Cold Park Wood

Scott Laithe

Bolton-by-Bowland

Rainber Wood

Bolton Park

Hartsails Wood

A59

Bolton Hall Farm

Skirden Beck

Docker

Holden Beck

Brownthwaites

Sawley Lodge

River Ribble

Abbey

P

½ mile

500m

SAWLEY
240ft 74m

81

The riverside woodland holds beech, oak and silver birch. The beech, 'lady of the woods', has oval leaves which are pale green in spring, dark green in summer, and orange, gold and bronze just before being cast in autumn. The fruit of the tree is a hairy husk which, in autumn, turns brown and, splitting into four, jettisons the triangular seeds, known as beech mast. In the old forest days, this provided a nutritious snack for deer and wild boar.

On the oak tree, the leaves are irregularly lobed. The acorns were used to nourish pigs which were admitted to parts of the old forest in autumn, the custom being known as pannage. The bark of the oak yielded tannin for dyeing leather. Silver birch, its bark white, with black diamond-shaped markings, thrives in the northern woods, producing an abundance of seed. The tree itself does not have a particularly long life, being prone to attack from fungus.

Primroses spangle the banks of the Ribble in spring. Foxgloves are numerous in the summer glades, and in the pastures are harebell, milkwort and tormentil. In some lightly-wooded areas, in spring, the ground bears the lush growth of ransoms, the 'wild garlic', which has a penetrating smell. The massed white flowers give the impression of a light snowfall. Look closely at a single flower-head, with its twenty-five star-like flowers.

After crossing a few fields, the path reaches a motor road not far from Gisburne Park. As related, Lord Ribblesdale was one of the landowners, introducing sika deer to his park. Animals were carted from here to the hunting area, the hope being that they would be recovered at the day's end to be available for another hunt. A stone building with entrances of appropriately small size was erected for deer.

Lord Ribblesdale had a financial interest in the local railway but, at the time of its construction, did not want it to mar his parkland, so a tunnel was made with castellated portals. The mansion in which Lord Ribblesdale spent his last days, lonely and disconsolate because of the death of his wife and of his son, Charles, at Gallipoli, is now owned by the Hindley family. This grade 1 listed eighteenth-century building has been extended to contain new and sophisticated medical services as a private hospital.

The footpath from Gisburn back to Sawley involves some roadwork to Park House. Follow the approach to the farmhouse and use the stile in the fence to the right, subsequently crossing a beck by a wooden bridge. Thence by field path via Fooden, near where the tang of sulphuretted hydrogen (a smell like rotten eggs !) comes from a mineral spring which was described in a magazine article of 1906 as being 'a kind of little Harrogate'.

From Fooden the path is at the rim of the Ribble Gorge before crossing to Scott Laithe Farm. If, on the way to the farm, you hear a shrill squeal, it might be the alarm call of the sika deer.

Brown hares inhabit the big fields, which have been re-seeded with rye grass. A hare is distinguishable from the rabbit because of its slightly larger size and the black tips to the ears. Hares lie at ground level rather than burrowing, as rabbits do.

From Scott Laithe, descend to the cluster of buildings which were once in attendance on Bolton Hall (demolished). Some of the outbuildings and cottages remain. The path lies near the gamekeepers' house and then follows a drive set between two lines of trees. The drive heads purposefully towards the village of Bolton-by-Bowland.

This village grew up at the edge of the Forest of Bowland, the boundaries of which later contracted. Bolton is architecturally pleasing, with two greens and some village stocks. The principal family for centuries was named Pudsay. In the second half of the fifteenth century, Sir Ralph Pudsay spent

The River Ribble near Sawley. No charge is made for visiting nearby Sawley Abbey, the monks of which had (according to reports) to cope with a succession of wet summers when the grain refused to ripen.

much money on re-building the church, giving it a lofty, ornamented tower.

Sir Ralph was thrice married and had twenty-five children, as can be seen with reference to carvings of the family on his tomb in the Pudsay chapel. He provided hospitality to King Henry VI who had been usurped and, at the time he took sanctuary at Bolton-by-Bowland, had seen his forces defeated at Hexham in Northumberland.

The king was here during the summer months, a time when the reconstruction of the church was in progress. It is believed that he influenced the design of the tower, being interested in architecture and familiar with the lofty, ornamented style favoured in Somerset. So the tower at Bolton is grander than for the average village church in Bowland.

Bridget, the last of the Pudsays of Bolton, died in 1770. The name Pudsay continued to be used as a Christian name in the Dawson family. The Bolton estate eventually came into the ownership of Charles Wright, whose fondness for horses led to him having two private coaches and the tackle to drive four-

in-hand, which he did, as the oldest of local people recall.

Walk along the village street and cross Skirden Bridge, which spans the beck of that name. Turn immediately left along a lane to where there is a stile (right) marking the start of the last stretch – rather more than two miles (3½ km) – to Sawley.

In the first meadow (left of the path) is the base of an old cross. Several stiles are waymarked using yellow arrows, with tracts of woodland nearby, some woods having rhododendron which is in full flower by early June.

Bolton Park lies to the east, across the beck. The wayward beck is frequently altering its course and is quite often deep, as those who use an old footpath from Bolton Hall to Hell Syke Bridge know.

A wooden bridge crossing Skirden Beck, shortly before its confluence with the Ribble, is used on your return to Sawley. Having crossed, you will see a stile between two white posts; another stile lies across the meadow, and after this a long stretch across the flat grassland is marked by white stones.

The heron stalks its prey in the shallows of rivers and streams. When at rest, the bird may be as inconspicuous as a grey post.

In some of the dykes, beside thorn hedges, the foxglove grows. Water crowfoot is in dense patches, rooting underwater. The plant sports white flowers in summer.

The view eastwards, across the Ribble, takes in a deciduous wood (one of the harbours for the local sika deer) and Sawley Lodge, near where our circuit began. Crowning the skyline beyond Sawley is the blocky form of Pendle.

Trout, even salmon, in the deeps of the Ribble may sometimes be seen leaping clear of the water. Birds of the riverside and local fields include sand martin, mouse-brown above and white beneath, being the smallest of the tribe which includes the swallow and house martin. The grey heron is unmistakable because of its size and prominent beak.

Of the other riverside birds, the oyster-catcher is a dandy, with pied plumage, red bill and pink legs. The sandpiper is a small, restless wader. Notice, as it perches, that it constantly moves its tail-end up and down and that when in flight the wings flicker, being held stiffly down-curved during brief intervals of gliding, in a way that no other bird does.

Near to Sawley, where reeds flourish near the bridge, the reed bunting is present. Notice the black head and throat and the white collar marking out an adult bird. The brown back is streaked with black. This bunting often flicks its tail when perched, displaying the white outer feathers.

At the approach to Sawley Bridge there is a thorn hedge, adorned (in early summer) by wild roses in flower.

WALK 13: STONYHURST AND KEMPLE END

Start: Hurst Green. Grid Ref: 684 382
Distance: 7 miles (11km)
OS Maps: Pathfinder 680 (SD 63/73) and 669 (SD 64/74)
Walking Time: 4 hours

This most satisfying walk begins with a stretch of roadwork in park-like country, with the eyes ranging ahead to the green cupolas on the towers of Stonyhurst College. Kemple End is a viewpoint for the Ribble Valley and the whole range of Pendle Hill. After a spell in the backwoods of Longridge Fell, the path descends through a Scottish-type scenery of pines and blaeberry (to use the Scottish name for bilberry), and the last stretch is along a path by a brook in a beech wood.

It was near Hurst Green in 1826 that a certain John L McAdam, who became so famous for his roadmaking ideas that his name lives on in the word 'tarmacadam', tried out new road construction methods. The village, with its air of antiquity, is a good starting point because there is space for parking in that part of the village lying at the approaches to Stonyhurst College.

Pass the Shireburn Almshouses (right), near the college gates. The almshouses were moved to this site, stone by stone, just after the 1939-45 war, having previously stood on the eastern side of Longridge Fell, where they were built by Sir Nicholas Shireburn in 1706. Notice, carved in stone, the arms of the illustrious Shireburns.

Now walk between the gateposts where the road enters the college grounds. A signpost bears the school crest. Immediately beyond is a sign proclaiming 'Forest of Bowland', with the now-familiar emblem of a hen harrier.

The road, having passed between stretches of woodland, bends to the right – and straight ahead are the twin lakes and imposing backdrop of the college. The Victorian chapel, its design based on Kings College, Cambridge, stands grandly to the right of the range of buildings.

Stonyhurst was inherited by the Jesuits in 1794 in somewhat sad circumstances. The mighty Shireburn family had a series of misfortunes. As Sir Nicholas supervised his new mansion in 1702, he received the heart-rending news of the death of his infant son from eating yew berries. Sir Nicholas himself died in 1717, and the property was inherited by his married daughter, who died without issue. The house passed to the Weld family, thence to the Jesuits. Among the famous pupils here were Sir Arthur Conan Doyle, the naturalist Charles Waterton and Charles Laughton, the actor.

The road to the college is as straight as an arrow-flight. Then it bends, in the vicinity of one of the two long lakes which add to the splendour of Stonyhurst. On the water are Canada geese and mallard.

Continue along the road to where a footpath sign (left) points towards land which is a golf course used by the Stonyhurst Park Golf Club. A stile is found to the right of the entrance gate. Follow the track, which has been reinforced in its early stages by brick, and head to the left of the small detached wood on the higher ground.

Descend to a stile to the left of a gate and enter a 'bluebell wood', which, in spring, is misty blue with the flowering of a plant which is much at home in Britain, with its moist and mild Atlantic breezes. The bluebells flourish between beech trees which offer an array of

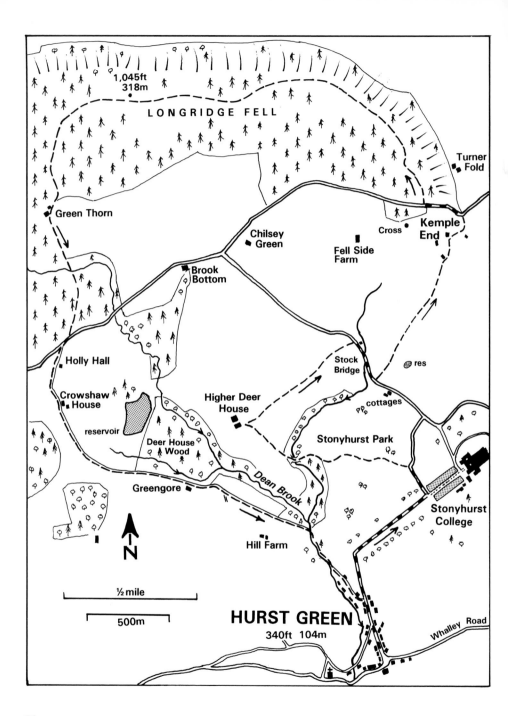

1,045ft
318m

LONGRIDGE FELL

Turner
Fold

Green Thorn

Chilsey
Green

Cross

Kemple
End

Fell Side
Farm

Brook
Bottom

Stock
Bridge

res

Holly Hall

cottages

Crowshaw
House

Higher Deer
House

Stonyhurst Park

reservoir

Deer House
Wood

Stonyhurst
College

Greengore

Dean Brook

N

Hill Farm

½ mile

500m

HURST GREEN

340ft 104m

Whalley Road

Stonyhurst College, a famous Catholic school whose 'old boys' include Conan Doyle and Charles Laughton.

bright green leaves in spring and, in autumn, has the spectacle of leaves turning orange, then reddy-brown.

Near the beeches, a new wooden bridge spans the brook. Head across the field for Higher Deer House. Go right along the farm track to a public road. You are in a country-side of large meadows and pastures, with many copses. It is stock-rearing country, where fields are sealed by gritstone walls, thorn hedges or wire fences.

At the road, go right, ignore the first public footpath sign (near a house), indicating left and continue walking on a narrow road fringed by hedges. Among the spring flowers are wood anemones. Look for a footpath sign on the left hand side of the road, near a barn.

The path, initially somewhat wet, is sunk deeply between a grassy bank and a hedge of gnarled thorns. Both the thorns and the worn state of the path give the impression of being old. The path had its maximum use when the

Shireburns were building Stonyhurst and vast quantites of stone, quarried at Kemple End, were transported this way.

These high fields hold nesting pairs of lapwings. The lapwing, also known as peewit (after its cry) and green plover (after its plumage) prefers wet ground where insect life is copious. The nest is a simple 'scrape' on open ground; the pear-shaped eggs being stone-coloured, though spotted with dark brown. In spring, the cock bird tumbles erratically towards the ground, pulling out of its dive when one feels it is about to dash itself against the ground – the dive being an outstanding feat of aerobatics.

The view across the Ribble Valley takes in Clitheroe at a glance. Pendle crowns the south-eastern skyline. The path reaches a stile to the right of a gate and is rejoined beyond. The sunken path now lies to the right of one made by farm machinery.

Kemple End is a collection of extremely

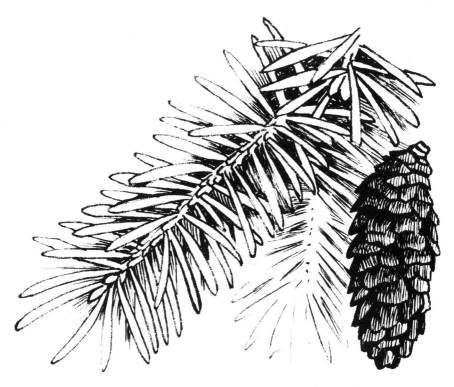

The needles and cone of the sitka spruce, the most common of the commercial conifers in an upland area like Bowland.

attractive farms and houses; it is also a quarry with a luxurious growth of moorland vegetation such as ling and bilberry. Kemple End is a vantage point for Ribble Valley and the fells of East Lancashire.

Turn left at the road, passing the sign 'Kemple End'. A small car park lies immediately beyond. The cross marked on the map, and standing in a field to the left of the road, is a large, thin stone with a hole driven through it.

Walk along the road, which climbs steeply. You will approach the back of a metal sign (showing a 1 in 7 gradient). Just beyond this

sign, on the right, is a track leading into that part of Longridge Fell owned by the Economic Forestry Group. The road, of 'quarry bottoms', gains height without causing undue stress, using broad zigzags and offering, near its highest stretch, a view of Ribble Valley.

Now settle down to a steady plod along a forestry road which is firm underfoot. (It has always been the policy of the owners to allow pedestrians access along the forestry roads.) The Longridge Fell plantations are mainly of sitka spruce, larch and lodgepole pine. On a warm, calm day the area has a resinous smell.

The trees stand a little back from the road,

giving some space to the ling and bilberry. Scattered about the property are clumps of old-established Scots pine which are an attractive feature where the bilberry cover remains. Some clear felling takes place and when the area is re-planted with a variety of species, the habitat will be further diversified.

Longridge Fell has a loop road with a viewpoint. Those who visit Longridge Fell specially for the view find this vantage point well worth the effort of climbing. The view takes in Ingleborough (north), Bowland Fells (north-west), Pendle Hill (east) and deep into Lancashire (south).

Keep to the straight track and eventually, at a Y-junction, take the left hand track and settle down to more steady walking, with the occasional cluster of pines to offset the effect of massed spruce.

The wildlife on Longridge Fell includes roe deer, with the occasional sika deer. The kestrel (also known as the 'windhover') is seen hovering, and you may be lucky enough to observe it side-slip and plunge to the ground to kill its prey, a small mammal or even a bird. As is customary with many birds of prey, the female is somewhat larger than the male. He is pale blue on the head, chestnut on the back and has a dark-tipped tail. The kestrel's call is a high-pitched *kee-kee-kee*.

The sparrowhawk nests on Longridge Fell; after much persecution in Victorian and Edwardian times, it is now relatively common and consequently some small bird species on which it preys are scarcer.

The short-eared owl, which is diurnal, may be seen by day, like a big brown moth, quartering the ground for voles. At dusk the *kewick* of the female tawny owl and the hooting of the male of this species give a sense of mystery to the area. A small population of red grouse clings to the more open areas of the fell where heather is to be found.

The walk on the forestry road ends just beyond a group of beating implements for use in case of fire and just before a forest road goes off on the right. Turn left along a peaty path between trees which descends to Green Thorn, a farm which has forest on three sides. The official footpath travels beside the farmhouse and across the field to regain the forest at a stile in a fence. The Brownslow Beck area contains some old-established beech trees and also having a little Scottish flavour in the presence of pine trees and a generous ground cover of blaeberry.

The path passes through areas where boots – and the occasional mountain bike – have churned up the ground into a porridge-like mush. At the road, turn right, then almost immediately left, for the last, languid stretch of the walk along a bridleway by Crowshaw House (where the farmer claims that 'Scotland begins just north of here') and Greengore.

Between Crowshaw and Greengore is an area of pastureland and rushes, with boggy areas: marsh marigolds brighten the wet ditches, and flowering gorse the drier places. Copses are seen adorning the gentle, rounded hillocks. Eventually there is a larch plantation to the left of the path; the trees are especially attractive as they assume new foliage in spring.

At Greengore, the name of which is said to mean 'green mud', referring to marshy ground, carry on down the track until you see another, initially covered with darkish pebbles, extending to the left. This is the bridleway and it leads back to Hurst Green via a beech wood, with a crossing of Dean Brook using a single-span bridge.

WALK 14: BETWEEN THE HODDER BRIDGES

Start: Higher Hodder Bridge. Grid Ref: 698 411
Distance: 4 miles (6½km)
OS Maps: Pathfinder 669 (SD 64/74) and 680 (SD 63/73)
Walking Time: 2 hours

The Hodder ('pleasant stream') has a rocky bed for the last few miles to where it provides the Ribble with an infusion of cold fell water. The Hodder also has some flanking woodland, with high-soaring deciduous trees to give a park-like flavour. Leave the car near the Higher Hodder Bridge (there is insufficient parking space near the Lower Bridge). Allow extra time to sit and stare at a grassy riverbank.

A couplet which is still chanted by the old folk in the lower Hodder Valley concerns three local rivers:

'The Hodder, Calder, Ribble and rain,
They all meet together in Mitton
desmesne.'

This is a lush, well-wooded area where the name Shireburn is still revered. This family is commemorated by alabaster memorials in a private chapel at All Hallows Church, Great Mitton (*walk 16*). During the present walk we think in particular about Sir Richard Shireburn who, in the sixteenth century, arranged for a bridge to be built over the Hodder. Now known as Cromwells Bridge, it is an astonishing structure – just a stone arch without parapets. Your view of the bridge will come when you stand on the Lower Hodder Bridge half way through the walk.

It is a circular walk, linked to the Higher and Lower Hodder Bridges by a footpath which samples both the wooded and pastoral aspects of the district. Parking space is usually available near the former. Space for vehicles is (alas) virtually non-existent by the Lower Bridge. It would have given a greater sense of adventure initially to have been able to walk up the valley.

The Higher Bridge is a fine viewpoint for the Hodder, Bowland's main watercourse. The footpath is just across the bridge, on the

left, and begins with a descent of stone steps and a walk on beaten earth down what in summer looks like a green tunnel of vegetation.

You will be mollycoddled on this walk, for it is well-equipped with what the planners now call 'furniture' – stiles, bridges, even long flights of steps with wooden framework and gravel fillings.

The deciduous woodland offers shade on a hot day and a sense of mystery at most times. Make the most of the Hodder in the early stages, for it is out of sight, if not out of hearing, for much of the way.

The old forest type of birdlife is here, notably the robin, its appearance made familiar by a thousand Christmas cards. The robin's sharp, sad song is heard in spring and autumn. The hedge sparrow, a familiar garden bird, is a typical northern forest bird. As you may recall from birdwatching at home, the plumage of the dunnock (to use a better name than hedge sparrow) is unmemorable, the main tones being brown and dark grey. The song is high-pitched and piping.

The big, dry woods suit the woodcock, which makes a nest among the leaf-litter and, when sitting, has such cryptic colouration it is virtually undetectable. An old gamekeeper used to claim he could locate a sitting woodcock by the sparkle in its eye. The bird feeds at intervals from dusk to dawn, flying to moist areas, where it probes the ground with its long bill, the end of which is highly sensitive to the movement of food-items such as worms and grubs.

A deciduous wood is carpeted in spring by wood anemone, the large white flowers being seen from March to May. They open or close according to the amount of sunshine which reaches them beneath the upstanding trunks of trees.

The springtime greenness of dog's mercury is welcome, though the plant itself has a fetid smell to attract midges, which are needed for the pollination of the female flowers. Dog's mercury is poisonous to mammals. On quiet banks, the primrose endures, its pale yellow flowers rising from a rosette of wrinkled leaves.

The trees seen on the walk are on the grand scale – beech, ash, oak among them – and also present are rowans which offer the late summer spectacle of red berries, which taste sour but are rich in vitamin C. Country-folk used to make an appetising jelly from them. The leaves emulate the berries and in autumn they turn to various shades of red. Holly has grown to a quite respectable size, whereas in the old forest the holly was simply part of the shrub layer.

Breaking out from woodland, the path follows a grassy riverbank, near stately trees and with massed trees across the Hodder. The familiar water birds are here, and you would be unlucky not to see a grey heron, standing by the river in contemplation, stalking slowly in the shallows or (on hearing your approach) giving a harsh call of annoyance and flying off between the trees, with its head tucked well back and its legs trailing behind.

The stretch of open bank ends with yet another footbridge and entry into a largely coniferous wood. The titmice are heard calling in the gloomy silence. In spring, a distinctive call of the great tit is like the sound made by a rusty saw.

Children enjoy the flights of steps which have followed the re-routing of the path.

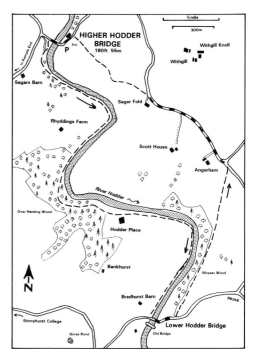

Counting the steps is a stimulus to a child's flagging interest. These woodland staircases also enable the walker to bypass a tricky area.

The final stage of the descent to river level is near Hodder Place, a mansion of a building with an enviable viewpoint. The hall was originally the junior school associated with Stonyhurst College and, after being empty for a while, was sold and converted into flats.

The path follows the edge of the river, passing also at the edge of a considerable stretch of pastureland. Near the Lower Hodder Bridge is a patch of Himalayan balsam (see Flora), which is 'spring-loaded' for the distribution of seeds. From the Lower Hodder Bridge you may scan the so-called Cromwell's Bridge (Cromwell and his men were in the area; the structure is marked on the map simply as Old Bridge).

Himalayan balsam, the seeds of which are propelled from the plant on hot days by a spring-like feature.

Rowan with its vermilion berries, a feature of Bowland in late summer and, through the autumn and winter, a boon to hungry thrushes, including fieldfares and redwings from Scandinavia.

Following the road left to just beyond some cottages, locate (left) the stile which marks the beginning of the walk back.

Keep near the tract of mature deciduous wood and savour the atmosphere of this mini-forest by following the path through part of Moyser Wood. The path eventually goes right to join the road for a spell, our route veering off to the left.

Two splendid features to be seen on the return are Pendle Hill and Kemple End. Pendle was a beacon hill, sending light to 'the Beacon of Sharpe (Sharphaw) in Staincliffe, near Skipton'. Harrison Ainsworth (1805-1882), the novelist, used Pendle as a setting for his violent tale *The Lancashire Witches*.

Pendle's flanks are weather-seamed, some of these gullies (cloughs) being caused by the

'bursting' of the hillside after particularly heavy rain. The sudden dramatic appearance of a torrent of water, spilling into the valley and causing devastation, was recorded on several occasions. In August 1580, Pendle seemed to leak in many places. In 1669, water pouring from the 'big end' of Pendle grooved the hillside and flooded Worston and Downham.

Kemple End, at the end of well-named Longridge Fell, is a contrasting landscape feature, being well-clothed with timber and having a much greener sward in the open areas.

The last stage of the footpath is along a well-marked path through tously woodland and then (away from the river) on a direct course which brings it out near the inn.

93

WALK 15: RIMINGTON AND THE SILVER MINES

Start: Rimington. Grid Ref: 806 458
Distance: 4 miles (6½km)
OS Map: Pathfinder 670 (SD 84/94)
Duration: 2 hours

During the walk, you will see the site of a mine which yielded silver as well as lead. The path lies near a bird-busy dam of a disused mill, and goes on to traverse several miles of mini-valleys with becks and deciduous woods. Parking is available opposite Springfield Farm.

The name Rimington went round the world as the title of a hymn tune sung to the words 'Jesus shall reign'; it was especially popular in the mission field. The composer, Francis Duckworth, was reared at Stopper Lane, which lies rather more than a mile (1½km) away.

The walk begins at the eastern end of the village, opposite the Old Manor House, where a sign indicates Twiston and a wooden gate gives access to a field. Keep to a central line down the field to locate the next stile, beyond which is a wet area where a few stepping stones have been laid.

Ahead can be seen Windhill Laithe (the laithe is a handsome barn) and you should aim for the right of it, where two squeezer stiles are to be negotiated in quick succession. Bear left and pass to the left of a remnant of drystone wall, after enjoying a splendid view of Pendle Hill, which dominates rolling countryside with mature woodland.

In the vicinity of Hollins Farm, the stiles are at the side of gates, the third such stile giving access to a field where the path goes southwards, not far from the depressions and grassed-over spoil heaps of the Skeleron Mine.

The veins occur in the Chatburn Limestone, part of the southern flank of the Clitheroe Anticline. As at Brennand in the Forest of Bowland, the veins which lay close to the surface had a high silver content. All lead ores in this country carry a small proportion of silver. This remains in the lead when smelted. It can, none the less, be extracted in refining, a method carried out in the Dales since Roman times.

At Skeleron (or Skelhorn), six veins were located on the rising ground to the north-east of Ings Beck, which formed the pre-1974 boundary between Yorkshire and Lancashire. (The mines are on the Yorkshire side of the watercourse.) The story of this mine has elements of romance. The ore carried twenty-six pounds of silver to the ton. William Pudsay, who, according to the historian Webster, in the days of the first Queen Elizabeth was Squire of Bolton-by-Bowland, and 'did get good store of Silver Ore and converted it to his own use (or rather coined it as many believe . . . which the people of that Country call Pudsay's Shillings to this day)'.

'But whether way soever it was, he pre-cured his pardon for it, and had it, as I am certified from the mouths of those that have seen it . . . so cunning are the miners that if they find any Vein of Ore that may contain so much silver as would make it a Mine Royal, they will not let it be known, but presently beat it, and mix it with their softer Ore, pretending the one will not melt without the other, being with them a common trick, lest their work should be taken from them.'

The law of mines royal gave the Crown a right of possession and the right to work all mines producing gold or silver in sufficient quantities to pay for the cost of smelting and

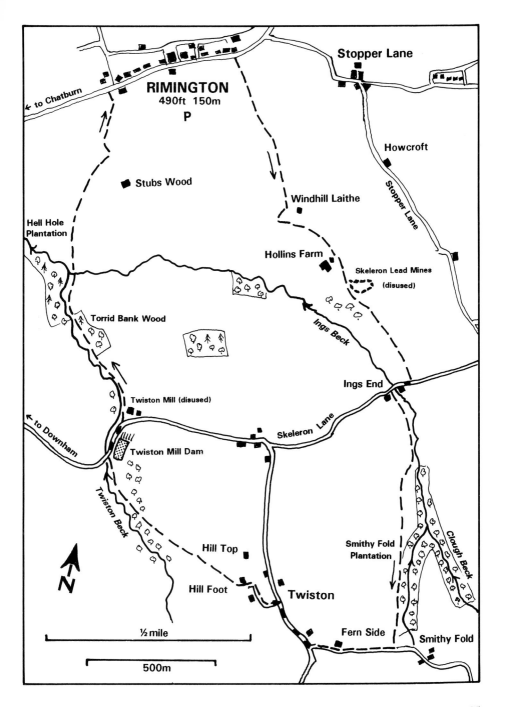

← to Chatburn

Stopper Lane

RIMINGTON
490ft 150m
P

Howcroft

Stopper Lane

■ Stubs Wood

Windhill Laithe

Hell Hole
Plantation

Hollins Farm

Skeleron Lead Mines
(disused)

Torrid Bank Wood

Ings Beck

Ings End

Twiston Mill (disused)

Skeleron Lane

← to Downham

Twiston Mill Dam

Twiston Beck

Hill Top

Smithy Fold
Plantation

Clough Beck

N

Hill Foot

Twiston

Fern Side

Smithy Fold

½ mile

500m

The delicate blue harebell indicates the presence of more acidic soils.

working. Pudsay should have declared his mine, which would have led to its forfeiture. His was not the only mine to be worked illegally and some owners, to avoid losing their mines, mixed the silver-rich ore with poor ore from neighbouring veins, smelting the two together as an ordinary ore of low enough value to be of no interest to the Crown.

Pudsay went further. He is thought to have set up an illegal mint and coined silver shillings marked with an escallop, which was the Tower Mint mark for the years 1584, 65 and 86. This story supports the suggestion that Pudsay was counterfeiting national coinage. No Pudsay shilling has been identified as such, for obvious reasons: every effort was made to copy the national coinage exactly.

The mines were worked fitfully over a long period. The latest attempt was made by a Burnley firm in 1920. After about eighty tons of barite had been recovered, work ceased.

In this area of great mining activity, summer plants include harebell, herb robert and thyme. The path extends beside a fence, but good views are obtained of a valley which was transformed by centuries of mining. The lowest of three veins is said to have lain below the level of the beck.

Beside the path is a quarry where the limestone bed is at an oblique angle. It was from this quarry that a man with two horses and a large cart transported rock for a new road at Barley. As the horses sweated profusely while drawing the cart up a hilly stretch of road, he allowed them to rest, one of the shafts being placed on the stump of an old thorn to remove the pressure on the animals.

Ings End consists of a white house called Mines Cottage, behind which is a small building which was a weigh-house during the mining days. A barn (converted into a dwelling) was once used by a lady farmer who had five acres (2ha). It is said that she slept in the space above the shippon. Heat rising from the cows kept her warm in winter.

Cross over Ings Beck and almost immediately turn left through a yard to a metal gate, giving access to a patch marked by stiles, the first being tucked almost out of sight under a thorn and the next two being close to remnant stretches of drystone walls.

In this well-wooded area, grey squirrels should be seen. The path runs to the west of the large gill down which flows Clough Beck. The woodland within the gill includes indigenous hardwoods – rowan, thorn and ash.

A stile is situated to the left of a gateway as the pastureland is left behind and a meadow entered. A gate gives access to a narrow, tarmaced road, and the walker turns right for Twiston, passing Fernside (1798) and turning right at a T-junction.

A local roadman used to say: 'There isn't much to Twiston. You might walk through it and not notice.' Take the first available left turn, down an unmetalled farm track leading to Hill Top and Hill Foot. Walk between the two houses to a metal gate, then make a steady descent to Twiston Beck. Do not go

The dam of old Twiston Mill is now fringed with vegetation, which provides nesting sites for waterfowl.

right down to the water until a step-stile has been crossed.

Keep to the left of a small barn and follow a path to a stile which is to the left of what used to be the dam of the former Twiston Mill, where the farmers had their arable crops ground. Coot and mallard are among the bird tenants.

On reaching a tarmaced road, turn right, then left, just short of the approach track to the mill. A stile indicates where the path lies. There follows a pleasant walk in rolling country, with good stands of deciduous trees. The woods have fascinating names – Mutton Acre, Torrid Bank and Hell Hole.

Just beyond this final wood is a plank bridge, and a track which leaves the valley (right), climbing a floriferous slope and crossing to a stile made of breeze blocks, the first of several which have small signs giving the names of the various destinations. Select the route marked 'Rimington'.

On the final stretch, move diagonally across a field, lining up with several buildings at the west end of the village.

WALK 16: EDISFORD BRIDGE AND BASHALL TOWN

Start: Edisford Bridge. Grid Ref: 727 414
Distance: 6½ miles (10½km)
OS Maps: Pathfinder 680 (SD 63/73) and 669 (SD 64/74)
Walking time: 3 hours

Park the car near Edisford Bridge, at the western edge of Clitheroe, for a walk beside the Ribble to Great Mitton. The walk continues northwards to within viewing distance of an old house where the Talbots lived in style and had their own retinue of trained soldiers. Unexacting walking throughout, with a more than average distance on roads. Yet the roads used have hardly outgrown their status of country lanes.

Near Edisford Bridge is a large car park, from which a short walk brings you to the river-bank, offering views of Pendle Hill and Kemple End.

In the days when there was a strong county consciousness, an osprey – the fish-eating hawk – was seen flying up the Ribble near Edisford Bridge. The boundary between Yorkshire and Lancashire runs up the middle of the river, so a record of that single bird appeared in the bird reference books of each county.

Follow the now-familiar Ribble Way signs – wavy blue lines – and if you go in high summer the riverbank (and a leafy division between it and the caravan park) will have an abundance of Himalayan balsam. This recent immigrant has colonised every untended

The River Ribble near Edisford, on the edge of Clitheroe.

space and will eventually be seen growing lustily from cracks between heaps of stone.

There being no right of way through Siddows Farm, the site of the old Kings Mill where local grain had to be ground, the path diverts to Henthorn Lane, which is fairly narrow and winding, with some mature deciduous woodland (right) and a household waste dispersal centre (known in the old days as a 'tip') to the left.

You do not actually see the rubbish because of an intervening bank, planted up with a variety of trees, including rowan and cherry. You do hear a chorus of cries from attendant gulls, mainly lesser black-backed gulls, and the air is half-full of them. They commute to the nearby reach of the Ribble to wash and preen.

The road now runs beside the Ribble, which here sweeps round a bend, with Kemple End to provide a 'backcloth'. The farm buildings (left) have a sign giving the name 'Fishes and Peggy Hill', which would appear to be a case of two farms amalgamated.

A second farm in this area is Shuttleworth, and you bypass the farmyard, the Ribble Way signs indicating a small croft with a sliding wooden gate at either end. (The toilets you see in the farmyard were installed for school parties on educational visits. They are not for walkers.)

Beyond are the Mitton flats [level ground beside the Ribble], with a water authority aqueduct providing a modernistic touch before you walk on through an unspoilt and contented countryside to emerge on the road near the Aspinall Arms. Turn right for Mitton Bridge – and what before 1974 was the far west of Yorkshire.

From near the Aspinall Arms is the best view of a limestone ridge, on which stand, by the right of many centuries, the Church of All Hallows and Great Mitton Hall, showing from this direction a gabled end, though it

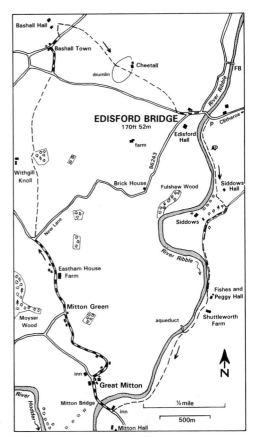

also has mullioned windows and enormous stepped buttresses.

The church is open to view on Sunday afternoon; inquire locally about the key at other times. Within is the Sherburne or Shireburn chapel, created in the sixteenth century to hold the vault and memorials to a family whose principal home was Stonyhurst. The Shireburn chapel stands on the site of the chantry of St Nicholas which Hugh Shireburn had founded in the fifteenth century. Sir Richard, builder of the present chapel, died in 1594 and is described on his tomb as Master Forester of the Forest of Bowland, Steward of the Manor of Slaidburn,

99

The redstart, seen in areas of old timber, is also known as 'firetail' from a patch of fiery chestnut. Only the male (seen here) has a black face and grey upper parts.

Lieutenant of the Isle of Man and deputy Lieutenant of Lancashire.

On the way out of Great Mitton you will encounter Mitton Green and Toot Hill (a former vantage point for observation). It has been theorised that hereabouts was the original village of Mitton. On ground near where a byroad leads off (left) is the base of the old village cross. Another cross was set up by the road near Withgill but, a century and more ago, the cross base (which was all that remained) was moved into a nearby coppice.

Our route takes in the approach road and farmyard of Withgill (a large group of buildings). Withgill was known as Crook until the middle of the thirteenth century, when Adam of Bury held forty acres (16ha) here, paying to de Lacy for their use the sum of four shillings annually.

Withgill knew wild times in the days when it was home to the Singletons. In 1461, the Singletons and their allies attacked the Talbots of Bashall Hall, to the north. The Talbots replied eight years later, when Alice

Singleton was slain, the weapon being a lance. It was recorded at the inquest that the lance had cost sixpence. In modern times, when Withgill was owned by the Co-operative Wholesale Society, a new farmhouse was built, the old house being converted into cottages.

Beyond Withgill, keep to the left of a wood. Stiles set in fences or hedges give access from field to field right up a road and on to Bashall Town. To the north is Bashall Hall. It is worth using the path beside it, returning to re-join the circuit, if only to sense the feeling of antiquity at this old home of the Talbots.

Bashall Hall, on the bank of a brook, has gathered around itself many tales of strife since, early in the thirteenth century, the manor was acquired by Thomas Talbot, a former constable of Clitheroe Castle under the de Lacys. As related, the Talbots and Singletons of Withgill were virtually at war with each other in medieval days, when it is apparent that the national law was not too vigorously maintained. In any case, it was a time when the House of York was in the ascendancy. The Talbots were Yorkists and high in royal favour.

The present Bashall Hall must have been constructed by the Talbots in the sixteenth century. One building appears to have been built to accommodate a retinue of troops – presumably the private army of the Talbots.

The Talbot connection ended in the following century, since when there have been a number of families connected with the old hall, which in due course became a farmhouse.

So via Cheetall to Edisford, where the hall which stands on the old Yorkshire side of the Ribble occupies the site of a leper hospital, founded by the burgesses of Clitheroe in the twelfth century and dedicated to St Nicholas.

WALK 17: DOWNHAM AND WORSAW HILL

Start: Downham. Grid Ref: 786 441
Distance: 4½ miles (7km)
OS Map: Pathfinder 669 (SD 64/74)
Walking time: 2 hours

Worsaw Hill is one of the prominent Ribble Valley limebanks (popularly known as 'reef knolls'). For most of this walk, the mighty roar of traffic on the A59 is muffled by hillocks and woodlands. If there is no room to park the car by Downham Brook, then cross the bridge, turn right into West Lane and, almost immediately, right again into a car park.

Downham, a village of attractive stone houses, green spaces and sparkling brook, has a huge backdrop in Pendle Hill. Downham Hall, which dates back to the sixteenth century, but with a Georgian frontage, has been home to successive members of the Assheton family since 1558.

Adjacent to the hall grounds and in a dominant position in the village is the fifteenth century church, the site of which held a much earlier place of worship, possibly before the Norman Conquest. Three bells and the font are said to have been brought here from Whalley Abbey. Notice the well-painted Assheton coat of arms at the inn. The Assheton family became lords of the manor in 1558, though the hall was rebuilt in 1835.

Ralph Assheton, who became Sir Ralph, was one of the first members of the Lancashire County Council and, being a director of the Lancashire and Yorkshire Railway, had a gold pass which entitled him to free travel. Lady Assheton helped to establish the Women's Institute movement in the county. Their descendant at Downham Hall is Lord Clitheroe.

Downham is lovingly maintained, and in summer the stonework is offset by the glory of flowers in beds and boxes.

The path begins near the car park in the village, where a short lane between two houses leads to a five-barred gate giving access to the fields, from which the classical facade of Downham Hall is in clear view.

Walk to the left of a wall, followed by a wood, then a wall, until Worsaw Hill is in sight. During this walk, several squeezer-type stiles will be encountered. Such a stile has three vertical stones, and you slither between two of them.

Pendle dominates the southern skyline. Its sides are scored with cloughs scoured by water. Brast Clough was created when the hillside burst open, disgorging a vast quantity of water.

Worsaw Hill, a Site of Special Scientific Interest, is believed to have held a prehistoric burial site. The limestone is rich in fossils, mainly crinoids, which are also known as sea lilies, though they are related to the starfish. These 'lilies' were animals.

The flowers include sheep's bit scabious, milkwort, eyebright, harebell and hawkbit (several species). Of special interest is the spring sandwort, with its small white flowers showing up where the plant is growing in clumps among the stones. This sandwort is a good indicator of land disturbed for lead-mining, for it is lead tolerant and thrives where most other species fail. The area was mined for lead 200 years ago, and efforts were also made at quarrying the limestone.

Among the nesting birds is the wheatear, at the vanguard of the summer bird visitors.

Downham village, owned by the Asshetons. The hilltop church (seen in the distance) holds many memorials to this illustrious family. The inn was named after them.

The cock birds are the first to arrive. Distinguishing features of the plumage are pearl-grey above and buff underneath, with a bold white rump. The meadow pipit, another nesting bird, is streaky-brown, with nothing conspicuous about its plumage. The song flight is a pointer as to the identity of the bird. The bird descends with stiffened wings and tail, giving a sequence of tinkling notes.

Worsaw End Farm was featured in a celebrated film, *Whistle Down the Wind*.

(If a shortened version of the walk is preferred, then follow a path northwards along the western side of Worsaw Hill, with the 'cement works' in view across the valley, and cross the line of the old Roman road and its successor, the Clitheroe bypass, to enter Chatburn.)

Otherwise, continue to Worston, through a six-barred gate, then a five-barred gate, to reach a bank of Worston Brook. The sides of this little watercourse are thick with vegetation and are well-sheltered by mature trees. Stiles lead the walker from one field to another. Latterly, a diagonal course is taken, leading to a (rather wet) lane which gives ready access to Worston.

This is a one-street village of fine houses, plus an hotel with the unusual name of Calfs Head. Fragments of old Sawley Abbey were incorporated in Worston Hall. An old cottage, Crow Hill, has a circular window at the front which was described to me many years ago as a witches' window, which is unlikely. The cottage is very old, and when a fireplace was being altered, clay effigies into which pins had been stuck were discovered. The witch traditionally associated with Worston is Demdike herself, but she spent her days on the other side of Pendle.

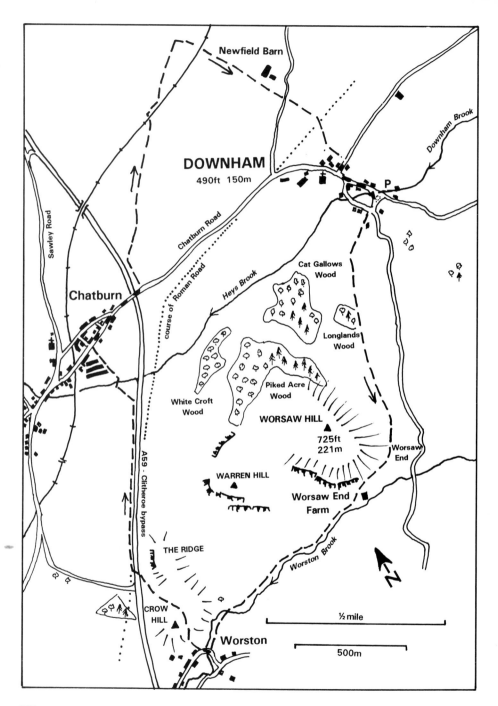

Spring sandwort, being tolerant to lead, is a prominent flower at old workings; these are not uncommon in Bowland and the Ribble Valley.

At the tarmac road, turn right, then right again just before the first building on the right. Near a traffic sign marking 'Bends' is a five-barred gate, leading to Crow Hill. Keep to the right of the hill. In a quarter of a mile, the path reaches the edge of the busy A59, the course of which lies close to the old Roman road. When the road from Worston to Chatburn was being widened in 1778, a cache of around 1,000 Roman coins, silver denarii, came to light.

Cross to a footpath which runs parallel with the road but, in summer, tends to have a jungle-like growth of briars, nettles, thistles, rosebay willowherb and rank grass.

It ends with a simple stile (left) leading you to a grassy area. Keep to the grass, passing a bungalow and ignoring a stony path. A path develops in the shadow of trees, with a step stile leading to a more pronounced path and, shortly, into the 'suburbs' of Chatburn. A former toll-house on the Skipton-Clitheroe turnpike is a shop specialising in ice cream.

Cross the high bridge over the A59 and then, noticing there are no pavements beside the road into Downham, avoid the traffic by a diversion into Swanland, turning left just before the bridge to walk on to a stile near a field gate.

The path crosses a large field. Ignore the metal gate. When the edge of the field has been reached, a simple stile leads into a wide gap between hedges. This, in turn, arrives at the railway, which is spanned by an iron bridge.

Just beyond, bear right and keep to the edge of the field, the footpath having become blocked by large fallen trees. Near a barn, a metal gate gives access to a lane which dips under the railway and leads to Newfield Barn. A gate to the right of the farmhouse gives access to a small field, thence to a small metal gate in a hedge. Cross the road, using a squeezer stile, and climb a steepish hill. Descend, with Pendle gloriously in view, into Downham.

WALK 18: CLIMBING PENDLE HILL

Start:	Roadside near Pendleside. Grid Ref: 814 416
Distance:	5 miles (8km), climbing 750 feet (230m)
OS Maps:	Pathfinder 670 (SD 84/94) and 669 (SD 64/74)
Walking Time:	3 hours

Pendle Hill, which was one of a chain of beacon hills, is broadly based, covering about twenty-five square miles (65km²) of country. Apart from the right of way to the summit, with a return on what used to be a road between Colne and Clitheroe, visitors are allowed to use a route round the hill and stiles have been fitted to walls. Wear boots, take waterproof clothing and, in winter, a hot drink.

Barley is a good centre from which to explore the Pendle countryside; it has large car parks, toilets and an information centre. Some people who ascend the Big End of Pendle from the south leave their cars by the road at Pendleside.

The ascent of Pendle Hill from near Pendle House is on a stepped path – Lancashire's most imposing staircase – which is something of a slog. In clear weather, you are rewarded, firstly, by a view eastwards, across the Lancashire cotton towns to the moors. From Pendle itself can be seen Morecambe Bay, the Lakeland Fells, Ingleborough and other bulwarks of the Yorkshire limestone country.

The reinforced path delivers you to within easy walking distance of the Beacon, the highest point, where you will meet a variety of people: bird-watchers, ramblers, joggers and members of the general public who feel elated at having climbed a mountain, only to discover that Pendle does not quite have the 2,000 feet (610m) necessary for mountainhood.

A beacon flared at the time of Victoria's jubilee of 1887, when twenty horses were employed in taking combustibles to the top of the hill. These included fuel provided by the breweries of Barrowford and Burnley – seventeen tons of coal, a ton of naptha and three barrels of petroleum. The horses used to transport it were normally employed on brewery drays. Over 1,000 people gathered on Pendle that jubilee day. It is related that free ale was available – at the bottom of the hill.

From the beacon, return to the point where you arrived at the skyline and cross the stile for a circumnavigation of the top of Pendle. (If there is a cold breeze, you will be pleased to learn that the route passes a splendid windbreak, which also has seats in the form of gritstone ledges.)

Robin Hoods Well is at the left-hand side of the path descending towards Downham. Robin, possibly a Celtic nature spirit who became a medieval folk, has given his name to wells and natural features – and pubs – in many parts of the North. Robin Hood was a relatively common name in medieval times. The Robin Hood of popular appeal may have been one who terrorised travellers on the Great North Road through Barnsdale, just south of Wentbridge. A Nottinghamshire Robin was glamorised by the songs of minstrels, by tales in books and eventually by Hollywood films.

The alternative name, Fox's Well, relates to George Fox, founder of the Quaker movement, who climbed Pendle in 1652. He recorded:

'I was moved of the Lord to go up to the top of it, which I did with much ado, as it was so very steep and high. When I was come to

Golden plover move up to the hilltops in spring and nest where the vegetation is not too dense. Look for the bird if you hear a low, rather sad, double whistle.

the top of this hill I saw the sea bordering upon Lancashire; and from the top of this hill the Lord let me see in what places He had a great people to be gathered. As I went down I found a spring of water in the side of the hill, with which I refreshed myself, having eaten or drunk but little in several days before.'

The rim of Pendle is a vantage point for features in the Craven district as well as in the Ribble Valley, which lies in detailed splendour not far from your feet.

There is now little heather and few, if any, red grouse. Within living memory, grouse were shot over dogs of the setter breed. The Asshetons of Downham and the Starkies of Huntroyde (Padiham) then had territorial claims on Pendle Hill. Edmund Starkie's lunches, enjoyed during a break in the sport,

were locally famous. 'We were always guaranteed a tip-top lunch and some old claret. But we had earned some refreshment. We walked a fair way in the morning and again in the afternoon', one of the party recalls.

The golden plover nests in areas of coarse grass. This plover has a gold-spangled mantle and dark underparts; it utters a soulful whistle. You may flush out a snipe.

In spring, a trip [small flock] of dotterel, one of Britain's rarest birds, has been known to linger for a few days on Pendle while travelling from wintering by the Mediterranean to northern nesting grounds. Two distinguishing features are white eye-stripes and chestnut underparts.

It was on Pendle that John Ray, an early botanist, reported seeing the lesser twayblade. Dobson mentioned two kinds of cotton grass, two kinds of clubmoss, butterwort and birds-eye primrose. Of special interest to early

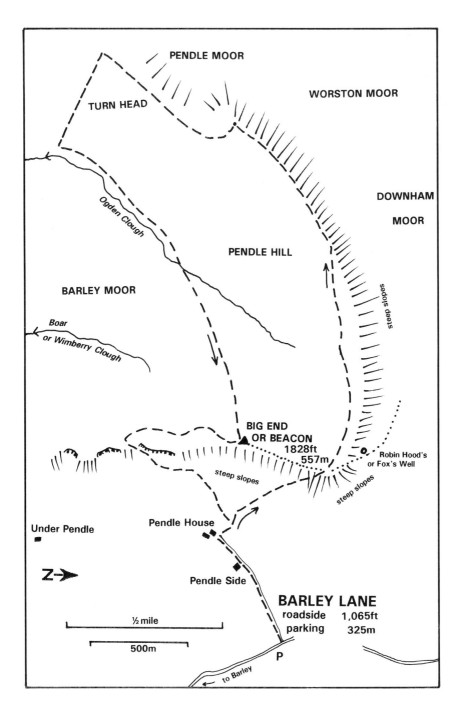

PENDLE MOOR

WORSTON MOOR

TURN HEAD

Ogden Clough

DOWNHAM

MOOR

PENDLE HILL

BARLEY MOOR

Boar
or Wimberry Clough

steep slopes

BIG END
OR BEACON
1828ft
557m

steep slopes

Robin Hood's
or Fox's Well

steep slopes

Under Pendle

Pendle House

Z→

Pendle Side

BARLEY LANE
roadside   1,065ft
parking   325m

½ mile

500m

P

to Barley

A stone trough at Pendle Side, with the Big End of Pendle rising beyond.

visitors because of its local nature was cloud-berry, which William Camden (1551-1623) knew as 'clowdesbery'. In 1700, a medical doctor who sampled cloudberry reported that it had a 'pleasant taste' and was 'a good anti-scorbutic'.

Clumps of bilberry give variety to the ground vegetation. Unlike other members of the large heather family, bilberry has no leaves in winter. The berries, much sought-after by birds and humans, are blue-grey from July onwards. Clumps of purple moor-grass are found in wet areas. The name comes from the purplish-green sheen of the leaves in spring.

And, of course, Pendle has patches of cotton grass, which is actually a sedge. The name comes from the flower-heads, which are like balls of cotton wool. White hairs develop around the fruits as they ripen. When the fruit is ready to be broadcast, it is borne off with the help of the hairs.

Walk at the rim of Pendle Hill, using stiles. In due course, reach a cairn-cum-windbreak which is large and well-made, complete with stone seating, a real haven on a day when the wind crossing Pendle has an edge to it like Sheffield steel.

Continue going west to a splendid cairn, tall, neat and solid, the work of the Clitheroe and District Scout Council, com-memorating Stanley Westhead (1910-1986) and Dr Y Hampson (a former District Commissioner). The cairn also marks seventy-five years of Scouting (1907-1982).

The path, which is on rough and tufty ground, passes round the head of a gill descending to Mearley. The cloughs of Bow-land and Pendle were created by a scouring of water on steep slopes. If you kept to the path, you would reach the Nick o' Pendle. Instead, leave it with a left turn just beyond a ruined wall, which brings you back to the area at which you will quit the hill.

The path is not the one you used for the ascent, though it eventually merges with it. Retrace your steps from Pendle House to the car.

WALK 19: BARLEY AND PENDLESIDE

Start: Barley. Grid Ref: 822 405
Distance: 4½ miles (7km)
OS Maps: Pathfinder 670 (SD 84/94) and 681 (SD 62/72)
Walking time: 2½ hours

This circular walk based on Barley provides double beauty, the hills being reflected in four small reservoirs – two taking water from Ogden Clough (which you will see on this walk) and two intercepting Black Moss Water. A track leads directly from Black Moss to Barley, where there is an information centre in which to browse. North West Water have issued a leaflet (available locally) which details a walk in the Ogden Valley. Another leaflet provides information about a walk near the Black Moss reservoirs, which begins opposite the post office along a track marked 'Blacko'. Inquire at the information centre.

From the car park at Barley, head westwards by Barley Green, where a tall farmhouse has a datestone, 1796. Nelson Waterworks transformed the district. You will pass the principal building, which dates back to 1912 and was extended in 1930 as more dated stones indicated. The filter station was made in part of a cotton mill (200 looms) which had been seriously damaged by flooding in 1880.

The initial stretch is along a road which climbs steadily to serve the Lower and Upper Ogden reservoirs, which have dams of stone-faced earth. It is related that many Irishmen were recruited for building the reservoirs, which supply drinking water to the Nelson area.

Lower Ogden (59 feet/18m deep and with a surface area of 21.12 acres/8.55ha) was completed in 1914. Upper Ogden (58 feet/17.9m deep and with a surface area of 7.014 acres/2.84ha) dates from eight years previously.

The dams were modified in 1991 by the provision of new concrete spillways. In their moor-edge setting, the reservoirs are fringed by bracken and heather. The crowing of red grouse may be heard.

The valley narrows. Plantations of pine, fir and larch – beloved of waterworks committees – are seen. The path which leaves the main route and descends to a outflow of

Upper Ogden Reservoir is that specified on the North West Water leaflet; it climbs the hill to the vicinity of Fell Wood and descends to the inflow area of Lower Ogden.

Stay on the main valley route to beyond the reservoirs. Signs indicate that you are on a stretch of the Witches Way. Ogden Clough is a typical water-carved valley, with gritstone forming low scars on the southern side and the higher reaches showing good exposures of the Pendle Grit of the Upper Carboniferous series.

This is acid ground, the vegetation consisting of some heather, a lot of bracken and cotton grass – which was the great peat-forming plant of the Pennines – in the moist areas. Mole heaps testify to the dark, damp nature of the soil at low levels.

Follow the Witches Way signs until, having used a wooden stile over a wall, the path – in its upward sweep – passes a cairn (left), just beyond which another path cuts right. Take this route, which will introduce us to Pendleside.

Notice the high gritstone walls, which are dark in hue. The ground sprouts rushes and coarse grass. The view opens out to reveal the Black Moss Reservoirs and, on a prominent knoll beyond, the form of Blacko Tower.

Many years ago, one of that vanishing breed – the small-time hill farmer – told me

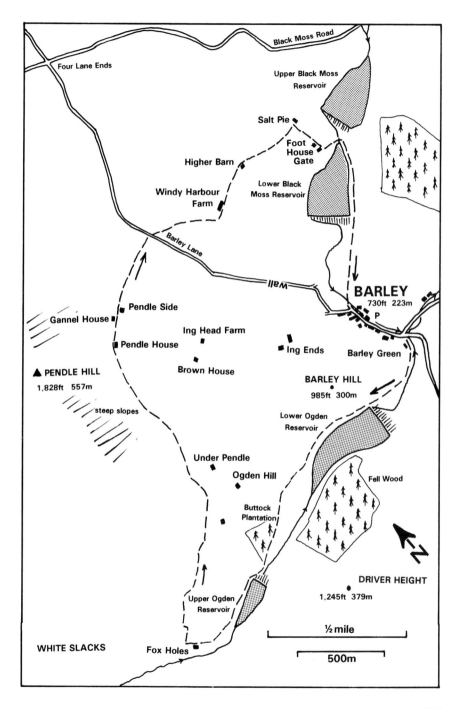

Black Moss Road

Four Lane Ends

Upper Black Moss
Reservoir

Salt Pie

Foot
House
Gate

Higher Barn

Lower Black
Moss Reservoir

Windy Harbour
Farm

Barley Lane

Wall

BARLEY
730ft 223m
P

Gannel House

Pendle Side

Ing Head Farm

Ing Ends

Barley Green

Pendle House

Brown House

▲ PENDLE HILL
1,828ft 557m

BARLEY HILL
985ft 300m

Lower Ogden
Reservoir

steep slopes

Under Pendle

Ogden Hill

Fell Wood

N

Buttock
Plantation

DRIVER HEIGHT
1,245ft 379m

WHITE SLACKS

Fox Holes

Upper Ogden
Reservoir

½ mile

500m

III

about the little farms along the southern side of Pendle Hill. A farmer might also be a handloom weaver, to augment a meagre living. Pendle Hill blocked out the view of the western sky, so if there was indeterminate weather at haytime, a man was stationed on Pendle. He waved a flag if a storm was seen crossing the Lancashire coast.

Those little farms, some of which are now in non-farming hands, include Buttock, Ogden Hill and Under Pendle. Further east lies Salt Pie, standing beside an old salt route from the coast.

Contour along Pendleside. Where there is a deep groove in the landscape, the vegetation has been bared to reveal shale with clay ironstone nodules. Pieces of shale in the stream which has to be crossed are seen to be quite large and dark.

The path reaches the motor road. Cross over and, bearing right for a short distance, locate a footpath which can be traced across country by Windy Harbour, Higher Barn, Salt Pie and Foot House Gate. The name Windy Harbour is believed to relate to an enclosure for deer, and Salt Pie is clearly a reference to an essential commodity for use in the kitchen and for preserving meat. The farm stands beside an old track and it is likely that the salt emanated in Cheshire and was transported by pack ponies.

The walker who carries binoculars will enjoy close-up views of the varied birdlife as fields give way to standing water at Lower

One of the two Ogden reservoirs, near Barley, from which water is drawn by the thirsty towns of East Lancashire.

Ling, the commonest species of heather, is empurpled with blossom in late summer. The red grouse feeds on the shoots of ling, and also has rich pickings at bilberry time.

Black Moss, the lower of the two reservoirs. In winter, scan the water for birds. One of the celebrities is the tufted duck, which dives for food and is swift and purposeful in flight. The drake, with its black body and jaunty head-crest, is quite easy to identify on the water because the dark feathers are off-set by white flanks. The Canada goose is recognised without binoculars because of its size and manner. Look first at the head and neck, which are black with the exception of white cheeks; the tail and wing-tips are also black. A species which was introduced from North America many years ago, it is now thriving. This goose has a trumpeting call when on the water and gives a loud honking in flight.

WALK 20: WISWELL AND THE NICK OF PENDLE

Start: Wiswell. Grid Ref: 746 375
Distance: 4 miles (6½km), climbing 800 feet (243m)
OS Map: Pathfinder 680 (SD 63/73)
Walking time: 2¼ hours

The last walk offers a contrast between a lowland village, once famous for its damsons, and an upland area, the Nick of Pendle, where members of a private club have a dry-ski slope (giving an alpine flavour in winter) and hang-gliders hover like multi-coloured kestrels.

Wiswell (pronounced Wizzle) lies far enough back from modern roads to have retained a real village flavour. It also has one or two wells. Springwater tops up the stone basins by the road. Local people tell you that the village name is derived from Old Molly's Well, which was later called the Wise Women's Well.

You are strongly recommended to walk round Wiswell before setting off on a round of Wiswell Moor. On the Whalley side of the village, a restored stone cross stands just over a wall, near Wiswell Old Hall, the supposed birthplace of John Paslew, last Abbot of Whalley (a man hanged in 1537 as one of the principal opponents of the Dissolution of the Monasteries).

This area reminds us of religious discord. Thomas Jolly was one of 2,000 Anglican clergymen who were ejected from the Established Church in 1662 because, on the restoration of the monarchy, they refused to subscribe to everything contained in the *Book of Common Prayer*. Jolly, driven from his church at Altham in Lancashire, was befriended by the folk around Pendle. The little Nonconformist chapel he established at Wymondhouses is roofless now but is still periodically used for services. The chapel at Wiswell has become Chapel Fold, now two private houses. A memorial chapel which bears his name stands in the nearby village of Barrow.

Being in a sweet limestone area, and sheltered from the worst of the weather, Wiswell's damsons were famous. An Edwardian writer mentioned 'the trees are white with blossoms'. Visitors speak well of food supplied at the Freemasons Arms.

Parking is possible by the through road, which is especially wide on the village section. Nearly every visitor comments on a magnificent horse chestnut tree in a roadside field.

Walk to the northern end of the village where Moor Lane begins. In summer, the footpath sign is obscured by trees. The old route to Wiswell Moor is now tarmacadamed and flanked by several big new houses. In early autumn, there is a profusion of elderberries and blackberries. Snowberry is a non-edible but showy fruit.

Near the topmost house is a field gate, and beside it a waymarked stile. Bear left after crossing the stile and keep to the right of the fence, gaining height quickly and being rewarded by a glorious fair-weather view of the Ribble Valley, from Kemple End to Penyghent and Fountains Fell. Within easy viewing distance are Clitheroe, Whalley and the Bleasdale Fells.

The footpath is not always easy to detect. Simply keep up the hill until, eventually, a wooden stile in a wall is in view. This serves a path which joins the one we are following. Enter clough country, the local variant being

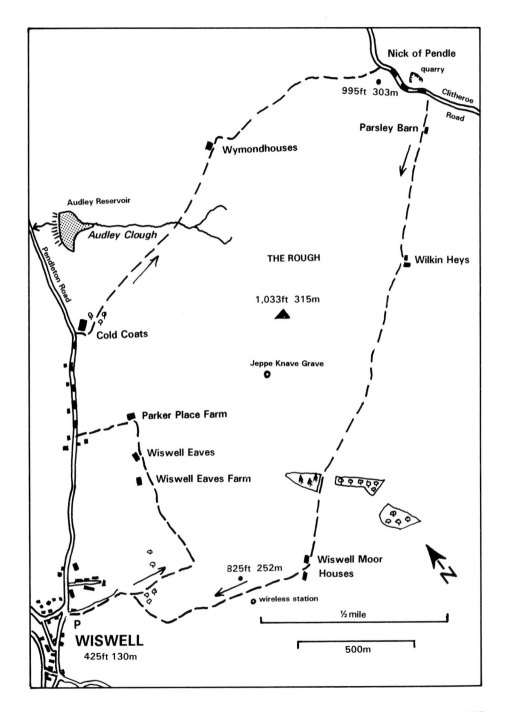

Looking west from the Nick of Pendle, a high road well-known to hand-gliding and dry ski slope enthusiasts.

short and deep. Your first clough is a V-shaped cut in the fellside, with some splendid exposures of the Bowland Shales and some ironstone, attractive to visiting geological students.

This countryside is also rich in indigenous trees – old oaks, hawthorns and rowans, which in early autumn have a profusion of fruit, the rowans having the bright red of the guardsman's uniform jacket.

A trio of farms snuggle at the moor's edge and the path runs alongside the buildings. It is not too well marked and you may have to resort to local inquiries. Wiswell Eaves Farm has an attractive old farmhouse and orchard within a drystone wall. At Wiswell Eaves the shippon (cowshed) has been converted into living accommodation and the big old barn transformed for modern use. Parker Place is

where you rejoin the Wiswell-Pendleton road.

This road is narrow, winding and flanked by trees which mingle their branches overhead, creating the summertime effect of going down a green tunnel. A footpath sign at Cold Coats directs you through the farmyard. Bear left through a field gate and look for another, which is painted red, thence across a large pasture. Notice the lines of venerable thorn trees, marking old field divisions.

The footpath crosses the field diagonally to a point near which two moorland brooks merge in a clough. The exit from the field – a track descending into a clough – is revealed at the last moment. The brook is easily forded, and beyond it the path resumes to Wymondhouses. You may see local notices

A song thrush feeding its young in a nest which is lined with mud. When the mud has hardened, a durable saucer-like depression is formed.

advising an alternative route to the official right of way, which keeps close up to the buildings.

From Wymondhouses, the route takes a comfortable gradient up to the Nick of Pendle. The big dry ski run near the hotel beside the motor road to the Nick of Pendle is in clear view and you may watch the activity. The Pendle Ski Club has two dry slopes close to the Wellsprings Hotel. Skiing instruction is available to visitors by appointment (tel: 0254 822347). The club sign features a Pendle witch with besom and skis.

Pendle itself is appealing to hang-gliders and the fliers of kites, so there is plenty of human activity to vie with the kestrel which hovers at a good height, its eyes scanning the coarse grasses for signs of small mammals on which it dines.

Probably the commonest bird on Pendle is the meadow pipit, which is often overlooked even when a cock bird does its best to claim attention by indulging in a 'shuttlecock' flight, calling as it descends with wings and tail held stiffly outwards. The nest is a neat structure made deep among coarse grasses.

Sabden, easily visible from the Nick of Pendle, has a church dedicated to St Nicholas – just one of the nineteenth century features of a community industrialised during the cotton mania. Sabden has a fanciful story of Treacle Mines. Over thirty years have gone by since I first heard of them and about the local people who wove parkin, using treacle as the warp and oatmeal as the weft.

Look from the Nick down the road and you will see (right) the metal gate which takes you on the next stage of the walk, along a bridleway to Wiswell Moor Houses. At first, the track is firm, serving the farm of Wilkin Heys. It then takes on more of a moorland character and there is peat underfoot. Eventually it is a track at the edge of grassland and near a drystone wall which, in places, attains a height of six feet (2m).

The Ordnance Survey map shows, on the moor, Jeppe Knave Grave. It is at the intersection of the parishes of Whalley, Pendleton and Sabden. Jebbe, who is said to have lived in medieval times, was so wicked that nobody would have his remains. Each parish took a third of him.

Leave the track just beyond the first house at Wiswell Moor Houses and head for the right of the prominent wireless station. Beyond, a stile in a fence to the right of a wall, and another on the wall below, set you well on course for Moor Road and the village of Wiswell.

SELECTED READING

History:

Mary Brigg, *The Early History of the Forest of Pendle* (Pendle Heritage Centre, 1989). A well-researched account extending from Norman times to the sixteenth century.

Stuart Crainer, *A History of Chipping* (Countryside Publications, 1986). A well-illustrated story of a fascinating village.

W R Mitchell, *The Lost Village of Stocks-in-Bowland* (Castleberg, 1992). Taped interviews, photographs and drawings give details of a community displaced in the 1930s by the construction of Stocks Reservoir.

Natural History:

Raymond Pickles (ed), *The Countryside Around Us: A Natural History of East Lancashire* (Lancashire Library, 1989). The area covered includes the Ribble Valley. Much of the wildlife content is appropriate to Bowland.

Walking:

A A Lord, *Wandering in Bowland* (Westmorland Gazette, Kendal). A meticulous coverage of footpaths, with photographs and a section with Ordnance Survey maps.

Gladys Sellers, *The Ribble Way: a 70 mile walk from Sea to Source* (Cicerone, 1985). Companionable as well as providing the essential directions.

Cyril Spiby, *Walking in Bowland and Pendle* (Dalesman, 1984). The author is a member of the Ramblers' Association and this excellent little book is not for the stroller but the true rambler, to whom miles do not really matter.

INDEX

Illustrations are listed in italics

126